THE MsTAKEN BODY

For Elias and Mina

THE MISTAKEN BODY

JEANNETTE KUPFERMANN

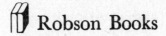 Robson Books

FIRST PUBLISHED IN GREAT BRITAIN IN 1979
BY ROBSON BOOKS LTD., 28 POLAND STREET,
LONDON W1V 3DB. COPYRIGHT © 1979
JEANNETTE KUPFERMANN.

British Library Cataloguing in Publication Data

Kupfermann, Jeannette
    The mstaken body.
    1. Body, Human—Social aspects
    2. Body, Human—Psychological aspects
    3. Human physiology—Social aspects
    4. Human physiology—Psychological aspects
    5. Women
    I. Title
    301.2'1   QP31.2

    ISBN 0-86051-082-4

Printed and bound in Great Britain by Redwood Burn Ltd.,
Trowbridge & Esher

CONTENTS

Introduction   7

1   The Mechanical Body   13

2   The Blurred Body   22

7   The Glamorous Body   39

4   The Polluting Body   50

5   The Birthing Body   66

6   The Ageing Body   85

7   The Depressed Body   102

8   The Abused Body   122

9   The Alternative Body   138

Bibliography   148

Index   153

ACKNOWLEDGMENTS

Grateful acknowledgment is made to the following for permission to quote copyright material: Wildwood House (*The Tao of Physics* by Fritjof Capra), Tavistock Publications (*Birth of a First Child* by Dr D. Breen), Millington Books (*Sexual Suicide* by George Gilder), Routledge & Kegan Paul (*Implicit Meanings: Essays in Anthropology* and *Purity and Danger* by Mary Douglas, *Children in Danger: The Causes and Prevention of Baby Battering* by Jean Renvoize), Weidenfeld & Nicholson (*Breakdown* by Stuart Sutherland), Peter Owen (*Sterilization* by Norman Morris and Humphrey Arthure), Oxford University Press (*Reasoning about Madness* by J. K. Wing), Fontana (*Child Abuse* by Ruth and Henry Kempe), Cambridge University Press (*Rethinking Symbolism* by Dan Sperber), The Women's Press (*Female Cycles* by Paula Weideger), Mitchell Beazley (*A Good Age* by Alex Comfort), Victor Gollancz (*The Experience of Childbirth* by Sheila Kitzinger, *The Wise Wound* by P. Shuttle and P. Redgrove, and *Male and Female* by Margaret Mead), Granada Publishing (*The Female Eunuch* by Germaine Greer), André Deutsch (*Old Age* by Simone de Beauvoir), Marion Boyars (*Energy and Equity* by Ivan Illich), Sage Publications (*Women in the Twentieth Century World* by Elise Boulding), Little, Brown (*Human Sexual Response* by W. H. Masters and V. E. Johnson), Jonathan Cape (*The Second Sex* by Simone de Beauvoir, translated by H. M. Parshley), Arrow Books (*The Facts of Rape* by Barbara Toner), Cornell University Press (*The Forest of Symbols* by Victor Turner), Frederick Muller (*The Male Menopause* by D. Bowskill and A. Linacre), Barrie & Jenkins (*Natural Symbols* by Mary Douglas), Penguin Books (*The Homeless Mind: Modernization and Consciousness*, pp. 37–38, by Peter L. Berger, Brigitte Berger and Hansfried Kellner, *Social Anthropology in Perspective: The Relevance of Social Anthropology*, pp. 133–134, by I. M. Lewis).

Introduction

'*I know no woman—virgin, mother, lesbian, married, celibate—whether she earns her keep as a housewife, a cocktail waitress, or as a scanner of brain waves—for whom her body is not a fundamental problem.*'

Adrienne Rich, *Of Woman Born*

For most women, the body is indeed a fundamental problem—just how fundamental is borne out by the alarming statistics on mental illness, alcoholism, gynaecological complications, rape and battering, as well as by the millions of pounds poured annually into beauty treatment, therapies and drugs.

The statistics show no evidence that so-called liberation and equal opportunity have affected the situation for the better; indeed, if anything, there is evidence of an increase in these areas in just those societies where women have shown advances in other fields—like employment—indicating that body breakdown may in fact mirror general breakdown in society, a theory temptingly put before us by Durkheim in the early part of the twentieth century.

Women's bodies, willy-nilly, constitute symbols of a most potent kind, and reductionist theories that ignore their power as symbols are inviting trouble. The result will be what I have termed 'symbol starvation'. Women's bodies then lose, as it were, their protective barriers, and become an open battlefield. The stereotypic whore/goddess gives way to the battered wife: Women, the Exploited become Women, the Drugged Class: elective Caesarian replaces 'giving birth', and early sterilisation 'oppressive' childbearing.

I have taken a circuitous route to arrive at these ideas on

the body: like most women, at different phases of my life, I have experienced my body in different ways, and each phase has brought its own level of awareness, its own insights as well as its own problems.

In my teens, as an aspiring starlet and model, I was initiated into the sacred world of the 'beauty-culture', and I observed my body almost objectively in a detached fashion, as it was moulded into an object of glamour. I was daily pummelled, pushed, tonged and tweezed, and certainly by today's liberated standards I was a sex-object, a dolly, who, passive, allowed herself to be primed and painted like a blank canvas every day by a team of technicians. At this point my only 'body awareness' was of my body's boundary; of shape and line, of light and shade; of creating magical auras with hair and gloss. I early on learned that the beauty-culture deals in illusion and myth, its aim being to transform the substantial to the insubstantial—to create the perfect incandescent image. Such is the stuff that religions are made of, and the commercial aspects are only secondary.

In my twenties, when I became a mother, I discovered another dimension to my body—its inner spaces, and biological rhythms. This is not to say I was totally unaware of them before, but pregnancy and childbirth has a way of dramatically and often rudely focusing one's attention on these inner voices; it forces every woman to confront her body in the raw, as it were—and certainly the handling many women receive during childbirth brings a sharp awareness, perhaps for the first time, of the body as a 'lump of meat', and of animal affinities.

Childbirth gave me an opportunity to learn a technique known as psychoprophylaxis which not only gave me some measure of control over my own body in labour, but which, as an approach to living generally, has stayed with me ever since, and which, combined with Gestalt therapy, I have been teaching women over the past ten years.

A third way of experiencing my body came through my

studies in social anthropology, under the controversial but always exciting tutelage of Mary Douglas at University College, London. Professor Douglas was most emphatic that ideas about the body always derived from ideas about society itself—for our attitudes towards the body in fact reflect something else, and that something is in society—whether these concerned beauty treatments, sexual mores, diet fads or whatever. She took as her basic premiss the notion that the physical body always reflects the social body, and is always used symbolically. I am indebted to her for many of the insights she provided. Later on, when I did my field study of a Hassidic[1] community in North London, many of her theories provided invaluable ways of organizing my material. The Hassidim themselves, with their sharp divisions between male and female, sacred and profane, taught me much about how the body can be used as a symbol, and how in fact this symbolism can *protect the body* from the sort of assaults I describe in my book.

The Mstaken Body is an attempt to share some of these insights, to bring together these different dimensions. There are, of course, many areas I have not touched upon, and many other lenses I could have used to view the body: physiological, anthropological, psychological and philosophical. I have written about women and their bodies because I simply know them better than men and their bodies, though some of my ideas might equally well apply to the latter.

Behind much of my writing is the growing feeling that the symbolic aspects of the body have been largely ignored or denied by the Women's Movement—hardly surprising, for the symbolic generally is disparaged and underestimated by all Marxist-inspired movements. Thus we have a paradoxical situation where in spite of an increasing spate of books, pamphlets, articles and manuals on women's bodies, women are being educated only to understand the literal, physical meaning of

[1] An orthodox Jewish sect originating in Eastern Europe in the eighteenth century.

their bodies, and to know nothing of their symbolic values. This has done women a gross injustice for, although they all now talk in the 'language of the body', it is a language reduced to a few stiff sentences, and the possibilities that the body as a metaphor provided, are increasingly less recognized.

If the Women's Movement has had little truck with symbolic systems generally, it has also relied heavily on mechanistic models of the body and has uncritically espoused technology and all which that implies. Mechanistic models, although useful on a day-to-day level, are limiting, and the new science of particle physics suggests that organic models may be more basic at certain levels. An organic model of the body has always been the cri de coeur of a large sector of the 'counter-culture' who ally themselves with radical thinkers such as Illich[1] and Schumacher[2], but the Women's Movement has yet to change its position radically on this point, and as long as it views Nature as something to be tamed and overcome, will stay tied to the technological view.

These are some of the themes explored in this book which is, largely speaking, an examination of the influence of technological consciousness on women and their bodies. Linked to this are other themes: the merging of the sexual spheres; the breakdown of mutuality; the lack of ideological backdrop against which to play out the drama of the life-cycle, and in particular the idea of Death as Nothingness; and how all these in one way or another affect the way women relate to their bodies.

A new mythology has sprung up which uses the language of the body; it has seduced many women who now use its vocabulary, but has created its own problems. An attempt has been made to destroy the symbol of women's bodies, and we

[1] Ivan Illich, see bibliography.

[2] E. F. Schumacher, author of *Small Is Beautiful*, 1973.

have been left with a physical husk and a lot of 'angst' that has no outlet.

This book is for the third wave of feminists who tell me they want to reclaim their bodies.

CHAPTER 1

The Mechanical Body

'*All mechanical progress is towards greater and greater efficiency: ultimately therefore, towards a world in which* nothing goes wrong. *But in a world in which nothing went wrong, many of the qualities which Mr Wells regards as "godlike" would be no more valuable than the animal faculty of moving the ears.*'

George Orwell, *The Road to Wigan Pier*

'*If it is only the body that matters, we might as well all commit euthanasia here and now. But people are more than bodies—that's the most important thing to know about life.*'

Mary Kenny, journalist, 1979

Our technological society has evolved a particular kind of consciousness, the essence of which is fragmentation, and this fragmentation is reflected in the way we apprehend our bodies. In primitive societies, where there is one over-arching cosmology or life-world, people place themselves in the world with much greater ease, and can achieve a far greater sense of harmony between their bodies, nature and society. In these societies there exists a cosmic connection between all things, animate and inanimate: no body exists in isolation; no single part of the body is viewed as a detached object per se: this applies to the healing of the body, its adornment and modifications, and to the enactment of body 'rites': they all constitute part of a greater whole.

In our society, the exact opposite applies: reality is organized into components that can be apprehended and manipulated in isolation. Medicine, childbirth, beauty therapy (especially cosmetic surgery), attitudes toward mental health, contraception and ageing, all reflect what sociologist Peter Berger et al. in *The Homeless Mind* call 'the tinkering attitude'. He himself warns that 'while the engineer has a well-tested repertoire of tinkering procedures available to him for the solving of problems in the manipulation of machines, such a repertoire is sadly underdeveloped when it comes to solving problems of the human psyche.' To that one should add the problems of the human body.

What exactly are the features of consciousness that are so intrinsic to technological production, and how have they affected women and the way they regard their bodies?

The first that Berger lists is *mechanisticity*—the functioning as a machine, with its correlate *reproducibility*—the 'nothing is unique, everything can be reproduced' principle. Add to this *componentiality*—the 'everything can be taken apart and put together' principle; *measurability*—'everything can be measured and counted'; and *maximalization*—the 'bigger and better', 'more and more cheaply' approach, and one has almost a complete guide to much of the advice and literature that pours out daily dealing with women's bodies, whether concerned with birth-control or this season's new eye make-up. Linked to this 'tinkering attitude', too, is what Berger styles 'problem-solving inventiveness'—the notion that every problem has an answer, and a complete one at that, if you look hard enough for it. This is part of a 'deeply technological attitude'—a carry-over from the toolshop and assembly line.

All these abstractions are perhaps nowhere better illustrated than in the assault on women's sensibility by the new 'sexocrats' exemplified by Shere Hite, author of the *Hite Report* on female sexuality. Like many contemporary women writers, she assumes that somewhere, out yonder, there is a 'self' that is waiting to be discovered, free from all social and cultural overlay, and thus she aims at discovering the instinctive as opposed to socially-conditioned, physical expressions of sexuality. As with many of her contemporaries too, the emphasis is on the *mechanisms* of sex rather than on meaning. Everything can be taken apart and broken down into units—orgasm, penis, vagina, breasts, friction, positions. Everything can be measured, from frequency of orgasm to shape and size of penis, and at all times a rigid distinction is made between mind and body—the physical and emotional.

Orgasm itself is viewed as a physical entity which has nothing to do with mind or emotion, and the more, the better.

The continual and earnest emphasis on *measurement* reaches unparalleled heights of absurdity in Question 10 (reproduced in *Sexual Honesty*):

> 'Do penis size and shape make a difference to you? What shape and size do you find are most compatible with your body—long and fat, short and fat, thin and short,' etc.

This certainly resounds with 'problem-solving inventiveness'. Just find your correct penis size and shape, and end of problem. At some future date, presumably, computers could be assigned the task of matching vaginas and penises for shape and size. The possible permutations provide for endless speculation.

Hite's mechanistic approach imposes false dichotomies throughout between 'physical/psychological' as, for example, in Question 21:

> 'Do you like intercourse? Physically? Psychologically?'

How, one wonders, are women supposed to differentiate?

When emotions are allowed to creep in, the taboo word 'love' is put in inverted commas, and the question is so loaded as to suggest that it belongs perhaps to the 'disease' category. Question 33 asks:

> 'If you have ever experienced something called "love" where emotions were involved, was it or were they a healthy or unhealthy relationship? How did these relationships affect sex?'

Throughout the *Report*, there is the dichotomy of physical/emotional with the latter assuming a perjorative 'female' value. Androcentrism is a feature of much 'liberated' writing from

Simone de Beauvoir to Erica Jong, where such male (i.e. superior) categories of 'having sex', 'screwing' etc. are imposed throughout. The toolshop is never very far away in such concepts as 'adequate lubrication', 'genital stimulation'. Other sexologists talk endlessly of vibrators (what did women do before the invention of the battery?), pre-orgasmic *workshops* and the like. I always thought a workshop to be a place where something was manufactured—both my father and grand-father had workshops in the East End of London where they manufactured clothing.

It may be significant that of the 2,000 questionnaires returned in the Hite Survey (out of the original 80,000 distributed) a large percentage came from lesbians or bisexuals, albeit recently discovered bisexuals. Anti-pornography writers such as David Holbrook writing in *Sex and Dehumanisation* might perhaps see in this one further manifestation of the 'schizoid' culture which 'depersonalizes sexual objects' by separating 'partial objects' (e.g. breast and penis) from persons, and which, in his terms, belongs to 'false male doing'.

His fears are echoed by the cri de coeur of one respondent in the *Hite Report*—a welcome note of sanity in the whole exercise:

> 'Well, you know, you've asked almost exclusively about *mechanics* of sexual experience: that was what you wanted to know, I suppose. But damn it, sex, like all the rest of life, is more than mere *mechanics*. Feelings and things as big and undefined and unwanted as "love" (whatever *dat* is) are the interior ocean in which we live and move and have our being.'

The ultimate mechanical body still perhaps remains the one described by Masters and Johnson, which totally denies an experiential core:

> 'Female orgasmic experience can be visually identified as

well as recorded by acceptable physiologic techniques . . . At orgasm, the grimace and contortion of a woman's face graphically express the increment of myotonic tension throughout her entire body. The muscles of the neck and the long muscles of the arms and legs usually contract into involuntary spasm. During coition in supine position the female's hands and feet voluntarily may be grasping her sexual partner. With absence of clutching interest or opportunity during coition or in solitary response to auto-manipulative techniques, the extremities may reflect involuntary carpopedal spasm. The striated muscles of the abdomen and the buttocks frequently are contracted voluntarily by women in conscious effort to alleviate sex tensions, particularly in an effort to break through from high plateau to orgasmic attainment. The physiologic onset of orgasm is signalled by contractions of the target organs, starting with the orgasmic platform in the outer third of the vagina. This platform, created involuntarily by localized vasocongestion and myotonia, contracts with recordable rhythmicity as the tension increment is released. The intercontractile intervals recur at 0.8 seconds for the first three to six contractions . . . The number and intensity of orgasmic platform contractions are direct measures of subjective severity and objective duration of the particular orgasmic experience.'

But as psychologist Liam Hudson put it in *The Cult of the Fact*:

'Bodies may look alike, indeed be alike, yet the contents of minds be totally dissimilar.'

It is time women stopped being blinded by mechanics and looked beyond the Masters and Johnson body, useful though their analysis may have been one on level: on another it has proved sterile and limiting and indeed 'no more valuable than the animal faculty of moving the ears'.

Just as technological style pervades and conditions our ways of thinking about the body, so does the bureaucratic—what Berger has called the other intrinsic part of modern consciousness. This is reflected above all in the 'everything has a name and place and appropriate agency to deal with it' syndrome. Thus traditionally taboo subjects ranging from premenstrual tension to death are aired nightly in TV chat shows, with the 'experts' on one side and the 'ordinary housewife' or 'sufferer' on the other, with appropriate telephone numbers to ring afterwards. 'Talking it through' has become the universal remedy for every ill. So problem pages, problem phone-ins etc. have greatly increased over the past few years. This takes us back to our 'problem-solving-inventiveness'. To talk about a problem is to solve it. But is it?

Traditionally the priest, as did the shaman before him, acted as more than mere ritual specialist: he was also counsellor, confessor, confidant, friend, father and guide. Modern psychiatry has attempted to take over some of these roles, but has scored very low on guidance, claiming as it does to be morally neutral. Meanwhile problem pages, agony columns and chat shows proliferate, attempting to fill some of the vacuum left by the disappearance of the priest and the lack of religious guidance generally. But again, because of their seeming moral neutrality, they are in effect unable to do much more than *dissect*. Thus, 'talking it through', 'becoming aware', are actually statements of impotence. As one counsellor recently put it, 'We lay bare the parts but cannot tell you why or how it should work.'

Marriage guidance provides perhaps the best example of this kind of 'ministering'. 'We listen, but we don't say anything.' The recent call in Great Britain for a Ministry of Marriage indicates the extent of the crisis, and is extremely symptomatic of the whole situation.

Traditionally, too, ritual proved a panacea and catharsis, coping with people's problems precisely through keeping taboo areas *undefined and ambiguous* and providing networks of supportive others in crisis situations. Birth and naming rituals, rituals marking the attainment of adulthood, weddings and funerals, all helped smooth the way as the individual moved through the life cycle from birth to death.

Traditionally the wedding brought the whole community into play. The costume, colours, music, festive food, all provided a way of saying something very important; on the social level it was the realignment of a social group; on the individual level it marked the passage from one psychological state to another. Wearing a white dress helped one achieve that state, for the dress was a symbol and as such was far more evocative than mere words. Today, attenuated registry office rites strip the symbolism and leave one with words only.

The Jews traditionally mourned ('sat shiva') on low stools for one week, while they were visited by friends and family. The sweetmeats that were brought, the mourners' unshaven, dishevelled state, the ritual form of address ('I wish you long life'), again all provided a special language which gave comfort because the symbol, as most symbols, was capable of saying more than one thing—of supplying infinite meaning to each individual. Without specified rites, few people know what to say to mourners, so they say nothing. But their feelings remain, their channels of expression blocked, dammed by the lack of expressive outlet.

Today, with secularization, the poetry has been replaced by prose. Ivan Illich warned us in *Limits to Medicine* of 'the language in which people could experience their bodies' being turned into 'bureaucratic gobbledegook'. This is nowhere more true than in the case of women and their bodies. With the lack of supportive ritual and symbol at the time of crucial life passages such as menstruation and birth, women are left with the formulae of the human engineers, who in their over-precision and increasing use of jargon and definition reduce all areas of ambiguity and complexity to arid definition. The increasing and more explicit use of language (i.e. *verbal* language) to describe and analyse areas of human suffering paradoxically *impoverishes* rather than enriches. Women are in fact being left *without a language*. Science may depend on definition—the human condition and its understanding depends on poetry. Because women are 'languageless' they are increasingly seizing upon gynaecology as a metaphor, and what is in fact voiced as a problem of the womb is often of far greater complexity.

It was Wittgenstein's conclusion that language could only deal meaningfully with a restricted segment of reality. It was always the part of ritual to acknowledge 'the rest which is silent'.

We are left with the question of what language women (or men, for that matter) have in which to express and apprehend their bodies. The limited vocabularies and styles of technology and bureaucracy all prove not only inadequate, but misleading and positively harmful in many areas: they detach us from a greater cosmological whole.

Unconscious levels that in traditional societies found expressions through symbolism, art, myth and ritual, special speech registers etc., in modern society may find all these channels blocked and may only discover an outlet, ultimately, in breakdown. This is the fate of the mechanical body.

CHAPTER 2

The Blurred Body

'*Then, in a flash, I perceived that all had the same form of costume, the same soft, hairless visage, and the same girlish rotundity of limb . . . In costume, and in all the differences of texture and bearing that now mark off the sexes from each other, these people of the future were alike.*'

H. G. Wells, *The Time Machine*

'*In the world of the future, parents may no longer worry about whether their next child will be a boy or girl: he may be both.*'

David Rorvik, *Brave New Baby*

'*What is . . . responsible . . . for the vanishing of "old-fashioned love" and permanent marriage is the masculization of women—and the accompanying effeminization of men. This Maleizing of women has been the most significant event to happen in my time, one that more than all the other "revolutions" has changed the vital qualities of our living.*'

Ben Hecht

On March 10, 1978, *The Times* carried a fashion article by Prudence Glynn which made the following observations:

'Has fashion ever been more schismatic? Spurred boots worn with peeping petticoats, men's tailored jackets with soft crepe frocks, men's ties with the sheerest satin blouses . . .'

and so on. The same evening I taught an ante-natal class, at which all the fathers (who are at these classes throughout) earnestly performed all the pushing exercises with as much effort and concentration as the mothers. My son that week announced that he was doing cookery and home economics, and my daughter that she was joining the football team.

Berlei, the foundation garment manufacturers, shortly afterwards came up with the news, after measuring 4,000 women over a two-year period, that woman's shape was changing from a curvy, egg-timer one to one closely resembling 'a thickened broom handle'. In the States, a similar survey carried out by Sears Roebuck, came up with similar findings, with women gaining inches round the middle while losing them off their busts and hips.

When asked to comment, Professor Desmond Morris, author

of *The Naked Ape*, attributed the changing shapes to 'changes in their life style'. As the differences in the life patterns of men and women have lessened over the years, so have their shapes. As men do less running and women less childbearing, it is only to be expected that their physiques should change.

Campaigns to combat 'sexism' have been in full swing over the past few years—from the cradle to the classroom, in families, churches, colleges, offices and institutions throughout the land, it has become the dirtiest word in the English language. Sexism in schools has received particular attention. One deputy head-mistress of a Hertfordshire school claimed in the September 1978 issue of *Spare Rib*, the feminist magazine that she had 'never for the slightest convenience divided the children into boys and girls, for any activity', but admitted that 'the boys love mixed netball and hate mixed football'.

Spare Rib devoted the whole of that particular issue to the problem of combatting sexism in schools, to the extent of providing a classroom poster that depicted 'feminine' woman's gruesome lot—i.e. two kids and a part-time office job, with a hint of Utopia in equal pay and training opportunities, alternatives to marriage and families, safe contraception, and free day nurseries.

Have chairpersons, Person Fridays, and (as regards my own name) Kupferpersons really augmented their total sum of dignity and humanity with their change of titles? This perhaps is stating the problem at its most trivial and banal level, but the new feminism is rife with such banalities. Feminism, too, operates at the level of semantics within a verbal matrix, because feminists have dismissed the idea of other languages.

What seems to be lacking in this whole approach which urges total elimination of differences and role divisions between the sexes, is any understanding of the nature of *exchange*, and what division actually does. Division serves a purpose.

Although there is a trend in Western society to minimize the sexual division of labour, this kind of division is well-nigh universal, and one might well ask why this is so. Put simply, it serves the purpose of promoting reciprocity and exchange, the very basis of the social fabric. The anthropologist Levi-Strauss in *Man, Culture and Society* states it thus: 'When it is stated that one sex must perform certain tasks, this also means that the other sex is forbidden to do them. In that light, the sexual division of labour is nothing else than a device to institute a reciprocal state of dependency between the sexes.'

It is this 'reciprocal state of dependency' which gets us into trouble—dependency is another word that is not liked today. It has been seen as part and parcel of the 'feminine' woman's attributes—dependent, weak, submissive, passive, inferior— opposite of masculine, strong, aggressive, active, superior. That 'dependency' should have acquired a 'feminine' perjorative meaning is again a distortion and over-simplification. Inter-dependency is the very stuff of all healthy human relations, and its unbalancing can result in conflict or neurosis, as studies such as that undertaken by Mabel Blake Cohen[1] show. In her study of fifty pregnant women and their functioning both pre- and post-partum, she examines too the role of the husband and the way his needs affected the relationship with his wife, and how that affected her greater or lesser neurotic functioning. Even more importantly, the study shows how dependency needs changed with the life-cycle and the various vicissitudes of living—especially during pregnancy and the post-partum period—and demonstrated that dependency was not a static concept that could be applied to one sex only. Her group of 'problem-free' women were

> 'mature, competent and quite free of conflicts about femininity. Whether they pursued careers or not, they and their husbands had established a relationship which was satisfying to both, not only sexually but also in their

[1] See her chapter 'Personal Identity and Sexual Identity' in Jean Baker Miller's *Psychoanalysis and Women*.

workaday living . . . We found the sharpest identity con-
flicts in the most problem-ridden group . . . it soon became
apparent that issues around comfortable acceptance of the
feminine role, adequacy of personal development, and
satisfaction of dependent needs were intimately inter-
woven and were of prime importance in success or failure
during pregnancy. Without due foresight, we had initially
focused our attention almost exclusively on the woman,
imagining that pregnancy had to do primarily with what
went on inside her. But the husband's part was forcibly
brought to our attention with our first cases and we became more and more aware of his crucial effect on his
wife's well-being. The issues which determined the
adequacy of his collaboration were similar to those in his
wife—namely, his feeling about himself as a man, his
adequacy as a person, and his handling of his dependent
needs vis-à-vis his wife.'

She adds that 'there is a tendency to overlook interdependency as a part of healthy human relations, both those of
husband and wife and also those of people in general', and
talkes of 'constructive mutuality'.

Anthropologists have always stressed the notion of exchange
as underwriting all social life. No human being is born totally
self-sufficient; having to look outside himself for the most basic
survival needs—food, shelter and reproduction—he is forced
to 'marry out or die out', in the words of Edward Tylor, the
19th-century anthropologist. For exchange to exist, differences
must exist too. Someone must have something I don't have,
and vice-versa, if we are going to exchange.

Exchange is not restricted to the social world alone. It
operates at every level in the natural world, as Fritjof Capra
describes in his beautiful and moving book, *The Tao of Physics*.
Modern physics reveals that all life is based on a system of
opposites and *their dynamic interplay and exchange* (my emphasis),

but that these differences and opposites are 'relative within an all-embracing unity':

'Examples of the unification of opposite concepts in modern physics can be found at the sub-atomic level, where particles are both destructible and indestructible; where matter is both continuous and discontinuous, and force and matter are but different aspects of the same phenomenon.'

Capra shows how all these concepts have been present in oriental mystical thought throughout the ages. They are present, too, of course, in Jung, whose work Germaine Greer dismisses as 'mumbo-jumbo'; in his ideas of the union of the male and female modes of our psyche. They are present, too, in the Kabbalistic writing, which forms the basis of the idealogy of the group of Hassidic women, and their tacit recognition of the male/female division.

To deny male and female is to preclude any possibility of interchange and to promote a breakdown of exchange at the level of the *body* itself, which is already happening in our society. We are the first civilisation in the history of mankind to attempt to eliminate all differences between the sexes. Different societies may have styled the male/female relationships in different ways, and as Margaret Mead pointed out in *Male and Female*, 'In this world, male and female roles have sometimes been styled well and sometimes badly.' But nowhere, and at no time before, has there been an attempt, as in contemporary society, to obliterate all differences of role. Mead sounded a note of warning back in 1962, before radical measures to de-sex schools etc., were implemented, when she wrote:

'Our tendency at present is to minimise all these differences in learning, in rhythm, in type and timing of rewards, and at most to try to obliterate particular differences that are seen as handicaps on one sex. If boys are harder to train, train them harder; if girls grow faster than boys, separate them, so the boys won't be damaged; if women have a little less strength than men, invent machines so that they can still do the same work. But every adjustment that minimises a difference, a vulnerability in one sex, a differential strength in the other, *diminishes the possibility of complementing each other*, [my emphasis] and corresponds —symbolically—to sealing off the constructive receptivity of the female and the vigorous outgoing constructive activity of the male, *uniting them both in the end to a duller version of human life* [my emphasis], in which each is denied the fullness of humanity that each might have had.'

She urges us to 'keep the differences', as 'simply compensating for differences is, in the end, a form of denial'.

But even Mead did not foresee that within a decade it would become not only a matter of compensating for differences, but a total denial of their existence.

Ten years later, George Gilder in *Sexual Suicide* described the situation from the point of view of the male, the 'sexual outsider and inferior' and 'chief perpetrator of social crime', whose only way of validating his manhood is through his role as provider, now threatened by the increasing encroachment of women, and the 'feminization' of all his traditional roles:

'From the hospital, where the baby is abruptly taken from its mother, to early childhood, when he may be consigned to public care: to the home where the father is frequently absent or ineffectual, to the school, where the boy is managed by female teachers and excelled by girls; possibly to college, where once again his training is scarcely differentiated by sex; to a job that, particularly at vital entry level positions, is often sexually indistinct and that may not even be better paid than comparable female employment—through all these stages of development the boy's innately amorphous and insecure sexuality may be further subverted and confused.

'In the end his opportunity to qualify for a family—to validate in society his love and sex through becoming a husband and provider—may be jeopardised. The man discovers that manhood affords few distinctive roles except in the decreasingly respected military. The society prohibits, constricts, or feminizes his purely male activities. It is increasingly difficult for him to hunt or fight or otherwise assert himself in an aggressive way.

'If he attempts to create rituals and institutions like the ones used by similarly beleaguered men in primitive societies he finds them opened to women. If he fights he is sent to jail. If he is aggressive at his job, he may be fired. Thus the man finds few compensatory affirmations of masculinity to make possible his expected submission to female sexual and social rhythms; and without a confident manhood he feels a compulsive need to prove it sexually.'[1]

How he proves it comes under the heading of rape and violence, and assertion through phallus.

Gilder's argument is, perhaps, open to the criticism that this definition of masculinity is still a very narrow stereotypic one. Equally, Mead still talks of 'the constructive receptivity of the female' and 'vigorous outgoing, constructive activity of the male'.

In their hasty recoil from any biological determinism, arguments fly back and forth about gender-identity, the universality of bisexuality, the cultural ascription of male/female roles, with

[1] The situation is not unique to the US or other capitalist societies. An interview by the author with a Russian academic made it clear that the same situation virtually prevailed in the USSR where it is exacerbated by an exceptionally high divorce rate, where a boy often grows up in a female household of divorced mother and divorced grandmother.

few taking any account of how any of these things actually affect the body. Dana Breen's important book, *The Birth of a First Child*, in which she looks at the various studies of the emotional and physical adjustment of women to childbirth, attempts just that. Rejecting all traditional definitions of masculinity/femininity as too narrow and static, she concludes that *only* a biological approach makes any sense. Thus femininity refers to 'those qualities which make for a good adjustment to the biological female reproductive role'. By this criterion many women exhibiting the so-called masculine qualities of courage, endurance, fearlessness and non-passivity, qualify, and indeed as studies show, make a far better adjustment to 'the biological female role' than the traditionally passive, dependent, etc., woman. It was found, for example, in a study by A. Nilson that women who assessed themselves as more masculine than others (with masculine here meaning strong, self-confident etc.) reported few psychiatric symptoms during pregnancy and the post-partum period, as well as less dysmenorrhea. Other studies showed that more active 'masculine' type women had fewer problems breastfeeding than their 'feminine' counterparts. There are, however, various possible interpretations of this. Psychoanalysts have reported, for example, that for some women breast feeding has a masculine meaning. But all interpretations seem to depend again on definitions of masculine 'activity' and 'initiating' as opposed to feminine 'giving' and 'feeding'. Breen herself admits that both feelings could be present in the same woman.

To Breen, then, the only reliable definition of masculinity/femininity is the biological one. But she comments on the reluctance of feminists to accept this definition of femininity, partly because of the 'inferior status' ascribed to what is feminine, and partly because of the danger that a biological approach could potentially be used in a repressive and reactionary way.

Throughout the book she calls for a redefinition of masculine/

feminine but, unlike the feminists, without losing sight of the fact that there is an ultimate criterion (the 'adjustment to the biological female role') by which to measure femininity. A more flexible and more dynamic concept of 'femininity' is needed, rather than its elimination all together, one where independence as well as dependence is allowed—indeed one that recognizes that the ratio of dependence to independence, of activity to inactivity, changes throughout the life-cycle.

> 'Femininity is not composed of one attitude, emotion, self-concept, but can mean different things at different times in a woman's life or moments in her life. To restrict the term as it has been done is harmful. One can only talk about masculinity in a woman when there is a sense of maleness (when a woman feels or fantasizes she has or wishes she had a male body) or when there is a wish to penetrate and impregnate.'

Breen throughout is concerned with the adjustment of women to the birth of their first-born. I maintain throughout this book that the increasing problems women experience with their bodies—and her statistics show that 78 per cent of all women have some problems around childbirth, whether pertaining to post-natal depression, breastfeeding difficulties or whatever—relate in some way to the blurring of the lines between the sexes, the loss of opposites, and its correlate, the inability to complement, or to achieve mutuality. I maintain that the loss of a woman's space is reflected in body-breakdown. In healthy human relationships there seems to be a natural tendency to divide into opposites—just as in the physical world there is a continual process of fission and fusion, of subdivision and unification taking place. As Teilhard de Chardin wrote, 'In every practical sphere true union (that is to say synthesis) does not confound; it differentiates. Evidence of the fact that union differentiates is to be seen all around us.' One study in Breen's book particularly bears out this thesis and points to the fact that in mental health (as opposed to illness) women always make their own space. She takes two groups of women, the one well-adjusted to pregnancy, and the other ill-adjusted. The author had predicted that the women in the well-adjusted group would perceive 'a greater dissimilarity between themselves and their husbands after the birth of the child'.

> 'Early in pregnancy Mrs Down describes herself and her husband similarly though she is more "reserved" and "understanding of children" than he is. After the birth of the child she and her husband are described quite differently. He is a "good mixer" and "not so children oriented": she is "more settled", "home oriented", "understanding of children", and "carefree with money".
>
> 'Mrs Marshall also ascribes to a traditional division of roles. Early in pregnancy when she still lives at home . . . she describes herself as "interested in the home", "likes to be at home" and "a person one can talk to". Her husband is "ambitious", "sporty", "aware of what is going on", "domineering", and "likes to go out different places". The descriptions are fairly similar postpartum but the difference between the partners is even greater.'

Several other case-histories make the same point. In order to function healthily, women have to create their own space.

In Rhona and Robert Rapoport's study of *Dual Career Families* there is evidence that even where husband and wife have achieved equivalence of work roles, at home the woman still finds it necessary to create her own space, in the development of what they call a 'tension line', 'which is set up more or less unconsciously between the pair and recognized as a point beyond which each will not be pushed'. This is often achieved by sharply segregating work and home roles, with the wife donning her pinafore as soon as she arrives home from her demanding executive role. This is true in many families where the high powered TV executive or architect, once home, becomes just 'mother'.

All viable marriages, and especially dual-career ones, have to settle the problem of division of labour. Many a marriage has foundered on just this point. Husbands and wives need well-defined boundaries. It is only with these well-defined boundaries that they will have anything to exchange, which is the basis of all good relationships. It is therefore meaningless to dwell on the number of hours a husband puts in with vacuuming, or whether he merely 'helps' with the housework or does it. The important thing is that he does one thing and the wife another, and they needn't always be the same things, although most couples seem to fall into an automatic routine: 'I do the cooking and he does the shopping' or 'I bath the kids and he takes them to school'.

Division of labour may change over time, too. Whereas a husband in the early days of marriage might expect to find three meals served up each day by the wife, he might be the one later on to open the can of baked beans or cook the special dessert for the dinner party. Whereas, too, it may be left to the wife in the early days to bath the children and see to their bedtime rituals, later on it may be the husband who is most closely concerned in the evening with their homework problems.

As to what the feminists ungraciously refer to as the 'shit-work' of the house, this presupposes a value judgment. I frankly prefer cleaning floors to sitting in traffic jams or queueing in supermarkets.

Bisexuality

The increasing blurring of the sexual lines is nowhere reflected as strongly as in promulgation of bisexuality as the norm. From pop singers to writers such as Charlotte Wolff, the message is loud and clear: Bisexuality is Beautiful—people who don't swing both ways are not giving full expression to the male/female components of the psyche, 'the one road to freedom as an individual', as one advocate put it.

A senior counsellor for the Albany Trust of Great Britain, an organization which helps those with sexual problems, in a recent interview said that she believed as much as 80 per cent of the population, given the freedom of mind, is bisexual—if only on an *emotional* level (notice once again the separation between mind and body). Certainly common sense and a look around society tells us that at the physical level (which after all is where it counts), the majority of people are still heterosexual. The inference 'given the freedom of mind' is interesting too, for it implies, as did Shere Hite, that out there, somewhere, is a pure sexual self, uninfluenced by society and its prejudices. But ironically the advocates of the Bisexuality is Best campaign make sure we are not going to be given any freedom of mind—thus any temporary identity problem is seen as latent bisexuality.

The Albany counsellor describes a typical syndrome:

> 'A typical example of bisexuality in a married woman would be that she may have married the boy next door, helped him with his career or business and had his children, who have grown up and left the nest. She now has time on her hands, time to be filled with either the cooking-sherry or another woman. Or she may have been used to giving and now wants to take.'

Notice how all the problems of middle age, meaninglessness, change of status, life-passage crisis and identity are reduced to the inevitability of bisexuality. Are there really no alternatives between 'cooking sherry' and 'another woman'? Notice, too, how the simplistic 'giving/taking' formula is applied, and the idea of exchange, of mutuality is denied. Similarly the idea is to pleasure one's own body, regardless of the enjoyment of the other, or as another counsellor of the Albany Trust put it: 'We

say that to enjoy sex, the other person must enjoy it also. And
men get hooked on the business of satisfying women.' (Dear
me, fancy 'getting hooked' on the idea of satisfying anyone
else!) He goes on to offer the following advice which is the
typical counsel of the sex therapist: 'Discover what you find
sexually arousing, what bits tickle, bits you like to be touched.
It is important to know yourself bodily as to know yourself
emotionally.' (Mind/body split yet again.)

When one unfortunate wife of a bisexual complains of her
feelings as a 'non-person' (and this is necessarily what she is
reduced to when there is no longer the possibility of exchange),
she is persuaded by a group set up to help such husbands and
wives to think of herself (and her perfectly natural and unhappy feelings) as 'jealousy', or 'fear of social ostracism'. Thus
the 'normal' and 'victimised' partner is stigmatised and made
to carry the guilt of the other and she is made to adjust to the
new normality of bisexuality rather than vice versa, and encouraged to correct her own feelings.

In an interview in *Woman's Journal* in October 1978, the
ardent feminist and psychologist Una Kroll stated: 'It is
perfectly normal to be bisexual; the conflict arises when the
individual fights his or her natural impulses.' Thus she is on
record as saying, 'I think that it is positively dangerous to one's
mental health to be afraid of one's own feelings. If one is
frightened of the truth, then one swings heavily in the opposite
direction.' She, in common with many radical thinkers, deplores any kind of value-judgment of sexuality, especially the
'growing feeling that to be strictly one thing or the other is
good, but to be a bit of both is bad'. But she does agree that
bisexuality, under prevailing social pressures, is an unenviable
burden to carry. Most importantly, she concurs that the
majority of bisexuals have chronic identity problems; they are
chameleons—alienated outsiders.

In all the writings of the traditional religions that stress the
male/female components of the psyche—i.e. Tao, Kabbala,

Hinduism—there is no suggestion that one should *physically* pursue bisexuality; on the contrary, it is expressly forbidden in, for example, Judaism. There seems to be confused thinking in all this kind of writing, again relating to static definitions of masculinity/femininity, for although the mystical tradition often cited by these writers acknowledges that God has both a male and a female aspect, there is no suggestion that human beings should blur the lines between them; rather that they should be aware of and acknowledge the existence of this duality.

When Kroll says 'There is good and evil; there is the image of God which is male and female,' she is stating an obvious truth. But once again, a literal, mechanistic meaning is given by the advocates of bisexuality to something symbolic. The androgyny of the traditional religions is part of their total symbolic system. Mircea Eliade writes in his classic study of myth: 'Androgyny is an archaic and universal formula for the expression of *wholeness*, the co-existence of the contraries or *coincidentia oppositorum* . . . to say of a divinity that it is androgyne is as much as to say that it is the ultimate being, the ultimate reality.' For the 'ultimate reality' is beyond categories.

Thus it was affirmed that Adam was 'man on the right side and woman on the left side, but God has cloven him into two halves'. (The *Bereshit Rabba* 1, 4, to 1.6.)

But this representation of the primordial, non-conditioned state was hardly meant to be interpreted literally and advocated as a doctrine for the masses. Equally, Jung's notion of 'animus' (the man within the woman) and 'anima' (the woman within the man) are symbols which express the relationship of the person and his or her unconscious mind, and again the notion of *wholeness*.

There was, too, *ritual* androgyny and ritual transvestism when roles would be reversed and men put on women's make-up etc. (even Judaism allows men to dress as women on Purim, the Festival of Lots), but this was always a re-enactment—a focusing on the primordial. It could be that the popularity of drag artistes such as Danny La Rue and self-proclaimed bisexual pop-stars like David Bowie, represent just that—the dangerous power of the ultimate reality beyond categories. The advocacy of bisexuality as a sexual norm, however, belongs to our impoverished mechanistic world rather than to the world of primordial myth.

The trend towards bisexuality follows logically from the questioning and break-down of gender identity. If there is no masculine/feminine how can such a thing as heterosexuality exist? (Or, for that matter, homosexuality—surely the 'homo' should have been removed some time ago?)

Its protagonists erroneously confuse the mixture of male and female attributes which every human being possesses with the actual definition of sexuality. As Kroll says, and no-one would dispute it: 'Within each human being . . . there is the capacity to love people of your own, as well as the other, sex.'

A question mark hovers round the word 'love'—if this means physically then we are back to Dana Breen and the relationship of masculinity and femininity to biological and reproductive functioning. The wish to impregnate is not feminine.

Where does one draw the line? Does one differentiate between emotional and physical expression of bisexuality? Bisexuals always make this division. Thus, one said, 'I love men's bodies and women's minds.'[1] Are bisexuals the victims of Cartesian (mind/body split) thinking in a puritanical setting? After all, in societies where male and female roles are rigidly maintained, women are often seen linking arms, holding hands, etc., and men kissing and hugging without any trace of bisexuality. Is it only in our society with its taboo on touch that this attitude could arise? Is it only in societies where men and women are naturally warm and affectionate to one another, where touch is not necessarily interpreted as an overture to sexual climax, that bisexuality is rare? Does latent bisexuality

[1] Quoted in a *Woman's Journal* article by Anthony Deacon, 1978.

really count? There is no physical expression of it—is it in fact just a handy blanket-term to cover *all* male/female identity problems and have we not mixed the sheep with the goats? Does this chameleon stance evolve because of *static* rather than dynamic definitions of masculinity/femininity? Bisexuality obviously can mean several things—it can hide homosexuality —the odd sexual wandering—flights from loneliness (which are not necessarily sexual).

Meanwhile, what one can call the trend towards bisexuality legitimizes an already existing identity crisis and breakdown of exchange. Its protagonists belong, with Shere Hite and the other sex experts, to the growing band of body mechanics who preach a 'servicing' of the body message. Polymorphously copulating individuals are isolated bodies with no complements, no exchange partners: they orbit dizzily in an empty universe. When exchange goes, every other human value must go too.

CHAPTER 3

The Glamorous Body

'We decided it was the quality of illusion, not just personality. After all, Hitler has personality, but you couldn't call him glamorous.'

Vogue, 1935

'Where there are no hidden dreams, glamour is hard to come by.'

Kathryn Perutz, *Beyond the Looking Glass*

'Glamour is a modern invention.'

John Berger, *Ways of Seeing*

Glamour, like myth—to which realm it properly belongs—has an elusive quality: few people would agree on its definition. The glamour of Garbo is worlds apart from the glamour of punk, but it is a misty and often distorting lens through which one views both phenomena.

The glamour myth in our society is all-pervasive: from the Libbers like Germaine Greer who decry the fact that 'women are forever trying to straighten their hair if it is curly and curl it if it is straight, bind their breasts if they are large and pad them if they are small, darken their hair if it is light and lighten it if it is dark', to the principals of modelling academies who are wont to declare from time to time: 'We're living in an age of laziness, there's too much freedom, glamour has vanished.'

Critics are apt to see either too much glamour—like for example, the critic John Berger, who sees it as a completely modern invention, 'the creation of others' envy'—or not enough, as with the school of beauty pundits, film critics and others who nostalgically reminisce about the 'grande époque' of glamour—the '30s and its stars. Glamour is essentially a style, and as Susan Sontag says in *Against Interpretation*, 'Every style is a means of insisting on something.'

What is glamour insisting on, and why has it become an

imperative of contemporary society, contributing possibly more than any other factor to the way women view their bodies and the sort of ideal types that are set up?

The glamour ethic is one of the prime reflectors of technological society—using as its prime carriers models, film stars, pop singers and 'beautiful people'. It follows, too, in the wake of 19th-century liberalism which believed man to be perfectible, a creature of progress. Kathryn Perutz in her penetrating study of life *Beyond the Looking Glass*—i.e. beauty culture in the United States—shows that it has virtually replaced formalized religion, having its own ideology, rites, temples, sanctuaries, high priests and vision of perfection. Through communications it unites women in a way no other comparable culture can or does.

What are the features of glamour that are so peculiarly modern, for as John Berger points out in *Ways of Seeing*, 'In the heyday of the oil painting it did not exist. Ideas of grace, elegance, authority, amounted to something apparently similar but fundamentally different.' There are, of course, still societies where glamour is unknown, where, in spite of bodily decoration, beauty is seen more in terms of modesty.

In the Oxford Dictionary sense of 'magic, enchantment . . . delusive or alluring beauty or charm', glamour has always existed and is found everywhere. This is not a particularly modern invention (nor for that matter is John Berger's 'personal social envy' which he sees as its determinant), so what is its peculiar modern quality that makes us recognize it in an Andy Warhol presentation of Marilyn Monroe?

Firstly, glamour in this sense is highly dependent on technological modes of consciousness—it depends again on the machine concept of 'componentiality', and above all on 'makeability' with its corollary 'problem-solving-inventiveness'. When Sheridan Morley in his biography of Marlene Dietrich calls her 'the greatest feat of theatrical engineering since the invention of the trapdoor' and Perutz says 'In the preoccupation with oneself as object, one gets the same pleasure and sense of achievement as in fixing up the car. One tinkers with oneself and beautifies it'—they have put their finger on the essence of glamour—the engineering or the tinkering attitude.

Glamour not only relies on artifice, on the unnatural (although there can be carefully contrived 'natural' glamour too —only, as Perutz comments, 'Instead of the usual hour spent in making up, you need two.'). Glamour also has 'reproducibility'—when Jean Harlow bleached her hair platinum in the '30s, it sent millions of other women in the US reaching for the bottle—it is not as easy to isolate and reproduce Mrs Siddons's charms. With the advent of the photograph it was possible to stylise, to emphasise one feature, one aspect, with a cunning play of light and retouch, that had never been possible before, and one of the essential features of modern glamour is that features—eyes here, a nose there, hair, breasts etc., can be isolated, singled out for the glamour treatment. The whole body is rarely important. Thus Marilyn Monroe has been described as an 'amalgam of hair dyes and plastic surgery', although Alexander Walker has conceded that as she progressed in her career she moved out of the realm of pure glamour to that of myth and incorporeality: 'soon she was slimming here, developing there, and, as her artistry increased, her form got more insubstantial—till in the end her hair looked made of spun-light and her face composed with an airbrush.'

James Laver, recognizing the 'machine' quality of glamour, called the camera the first 'engine for imposing types of beauty'. 'Ideal type' depended on one or more features being picked out and exaggerated through the camera's eye. Thus with Dietrich it was plucked eyebrows and sucked-in cheeks: Garbo —hollowed eye-sockets and plucked eyebrows, Crawford, the bow-tie mouth, Harlow, platinum hair, Katharine Hepburn, red curls and freckles, and so on. After Mark I came a host of cheaper imitations from the production lines of the Hollywood Dream Factory. Hollywood, too, invented such artificial additions to the baby as false fingernails and eyelashes, as well as virtually providing the inspiration and know-how of the newly evolved cosmetic industry. As the '30s advanced, women now looked to the movie capital and its stars for the new look, rather than to the world of stage and society. In a beauty feature in *Vogue* in January 1938 entitled 'Seven Steps to Stardom', an ordinary girl is transformed into a Glamour Girl, and the whole art of making-up has not changed that much since those early days:

> 'First, a foundation of greasepaint over the face, with a streak of darker greasepaint narrowing the jaw, then blended eye-shadows hollowing the eyes. Eyebrow pencil fines the browline, powder and rouge are brushed on and off again with a soft brush, lashes are blackened with mascara and thickened with artificial eyelashes. Finally, the mouth is defined with a pencil line and filled in with lipstick or lip-rouge. *In this way, glamour was thoroughly analysed and its effects calculated.*'

It was left to Howard Hughes back at the drawing board in his aircraft factory to design a bra for Jane Russell to get 'more production out of her bust' and Hollywood gave us 'uplift' too.

A star depended on her make-up man, director, and often lighting director (as he was the magician who could create the luminous interplay of shadow and light) to 'create her'. Every major star of the '30s had a complete 'make-over' job done by one or other of these technicians; just as in the ancient Celtic myth Blodcuwcdd was created from flowers by the magician, so we have the Svengali aspect of Garbo and Mauritz Stiller; Dietrich and Josef von Sternberg. Both women, awkward and lumpish at the start of their careers, emerged as incandescent, svelte goddesses after the make-over. The make-over soon became blue-printed for the average woman, too, and still remains beloved of women's magazines. Later on Vadim effected the same transformation with Bardot, and 'God created Woman'.

'Make-overs,' writes Perutz, 'show how any girl in America can be transformed through make-up, hair style and clothes into someone beautiful, charming and, most importantly, successful.' 'Why do they want to be made over?' asked one former beauty editor. 'Well, it's a fairy tale—that she would get a prince, or that she would get a better job or that she would just look better.' She is given instant class—chic—and also snippets of culture to make her instantly interesting.

Models are another example of how the 'makeability' concept is applied. The best models are always those with the *least* faces—i.e. those who start with blank canvases that can be filled-in with whatever look is current. I remember this from my own days in the business. I would marvel (and secretly envy) the skinny, mouse-haired girls, with their washed-out skins, albino eyelashes, non-existent noses and mouths, who would arrive at the studios in the morning with their fishing-tackle boxes full of crayons and paint, and emerge half an hour later with full scarlet lips, enormous Norman Rockwell eyes spiked with eyelashes, heads a-tumble with manes of curls, luminous porcelain skins—perfect facsimiles of Rita Hayworth, Mata-Hari or Baby Jane Holzer. The less definition one had originally in the face, the more potential there was for the make-over. Thus it was hardly surprising that the girls with the more 'foetal' looks gained the most ouststanding success.

Technology, then, created its own goddesses to carry its messages. Magazines and the model took over from the movie queens in glamour promotion; but the photograph and camera reigned supreme, reaching its apotheosis in the '60s when, according to *Vogue* (September 1978 issue):

> 'Everyone was trying to look like a photograph, as smooth and as flat as a page in a magazine. A doctor gave in-jections made from the urine of pregnant cows, someone

in Paris had a formula for getting rid of cellulite that required months of painful injections. Models thought nothing of having teeth removed to make their cheek-bones more salient, or giving up smoking because of what it did to their skins. The flat angularity of the girl on the page was the goal.'

A new make-up was invented by Mary Quant that actually imitated the camera's effect with light (cheek-gloss—a thick opalescent substance), for 'everyone wanted to catch the light', because light and its magic are the very essence of glamour and this is why, even more than the invention of the stage footlight, it took the arrival of the camera before modern glamour could evolve. 'Social envy' has less to do with it than *light*. Light, properly used, can produce an illusion of in-corporeality—of immortality itself. This is why glamour belongs to the same shadowy realm as myth, dealing as it does with the paradoxes of substance and form, light and shade, life and death. Photographs quickly become icons: witness the face of Garbo, 'perfect and ephemeral', the 'totem-like counten-ance', according to Roland Barthes' *Mythologies*.

Though glamour today may be far removed from the mystery and distance of Garbo, it lives on just as myth does as a sort of 'second-hand speech', in Barthes' phrase; just as any-thing can be myth, so anything can be glamorous; witness, for example, punk, a style which depends on presenting a ritually mutilated and tortured body to the world—on the 'displace-ment' of dirt (the ideal punk hairstyle requires that the hair be left matted, dirty and unwashed for months, preferably with cold cream or lard rubbed into it)—and which epitomises glamour for many. 'Dirt,' says Mary Douglas, following on from George Bernard Shaw, 'is matter out of place.' 'Matter out of place' is what punk is all about.

Critics may identify the resurgence of 'natural' or 'health' cults with the death of glamour. Nothing could be further from the truth. Although, by definition, glamour implies artifice and 'makeability', it constantly changes its relationship to the natural, sometimes almost totally incorporating it. In this respect, as well as in others, the '70s closely resemble the '30s, with the emphasis on physical fitness, jogging, health-foods and natural beauty aids. Miles of white fox fur co-existed with Tyrolean hiking holidays, dirndl skirts and Swedish exercises in the '30s; slimming, 'Buddha' exercises, bicycling crazes, eating nuts and dancing lessons were all the rage then, as now.

America, and especially California, has always been closer to 'natural' glamour than to more obviously artificial glamour, as *Vogue* explained: 'Exercise, fresh air, sport and bran, molasses, the mucus-free diet, the vegetable diet and the Biele total diet occupied American girls while English girls were still putting Biba brown on their cheeks.' But the concept of 'makeability' is still there: the creation of the 'natural' girl, the 'real' girl, the 'sincere' girl, the 'scrubbed from head to toe' girl, depends just as much on a production line approach as a full-blown punk.

Feminists have not appreciated glamour as part of a total symbolic system—just as they tend to underplay symbolism generally. Thus Germaine Greer in *The Female Eunuch* complains that 'Women are so brainwashed about the physical image that they should have that, despite popular fiction on the point, they rarely undress with éclat. They are often apologetic about their bodies, considered in relation to that plastic object of desire whose image is radiated through the media.' She observes correctly the 'dissatisfaction with the body as it is, and, an insistent desire that it be otherwise, not natural but controlled, fabricated.'

She writes of the myth: 'Her glossy lips and matt complexion, her unfocused eyes and flawless fingers, her extraordinary hair all floating and shining, curling and gleaming' and recognizes too that they 'reveal the (inhuman) triumph of cosmetics, lighting, focusing and printing, cropping and composition'.

But she does not understand the workings of myth. Greer disparages the 'Eternal Feminine', the idol, formed of concatenations of lines and masses, and recognizes, again correctly, that the *mythical* woman's 'essential quality is castratedness'. But in common with many other liberated writers she confuses myth and reality, not recognizing the function of the latter's 'Neither-Nor' quality (the mythical woman is *always* ambiguous in her sex—take Garbo—take Dietrich—and take Greer herself—a potent mixture of male stature and female hair. Greer is 'sick of the masquerade', sick of being 'a female impersonator' (the term is telling, and speaks of severe identity problems), sick of myth itself, for myth provides no answers; it merely re-states ambiguities and in one sense makes them bearable. We live and we die, we pass from youth to old age. We are patently creatures of manifest imperfection. Myth says we can be perfect, we can conquer old age and we can escape the burdens of our sex. In one sense we are all sick of myth because it implies paradoxically that *nothing can ever be perfect*, rather than vice versa. Glamour, like myth, does not die; it provides a never-never land where some of life's most tragic ambiguities and paradoxes can be mediated (ageing, for example). Those who see it only as a commercial confidence trick fail to recognize its myth-like qualities—its quest for an Eternal. But to see it only as myth is to miss its essentially modern components, its deeply technological features, and its role as a prime carrier of the message of 'makeability'.

Glamour refuses to die, because it is unlikely that in a modern world, without an overarching spiritual framework, man will ever be reconciled to his own death. It is ironic, but to be expected, that the only women who escape the glamour myth are those who live beneath the umbrella of an alternative, overriding religious ideology or who have entered, as in madness, into a private separate reality, whose basic paradigms differ from those of the technological society. In these societies, sagging breasts and bellies, wrinkles and crowsfeet, are not seen as threats: in these societies, where child-bearing and motherhood are at a premium, where breasts and wombs are not divorced from their natural function, glamour does not exist. Adornment, yes; elegance, yes—but glamour, no.

There are few women who succeed (or would want to) in making no symbolic statements about themselves through style either in hair, dress or make-up. Women's Libbers themselves certainly don't aspire to be style-less. Think of Gloria Steinem's streaked hair, Midge Mackenzie's hats, or even Germaine's frizz. There are some, however, who escape from the glamour myth: the first are those women who are so depressed or mentally ill that, willy-nilly, the 'natural' look of unkempt hair, long uncut fingernails and neglected grey skins takes over—and those who have visited psychiatric institutions will recognize the bleak picture. Now these women are out of touch with the world—in fact one tested way of helping to 'bring them back' is via the beauty culture. A new hairdo and lipstick has been known to do more for these women than a month's chemotherapy, for by helping them to use symbols again—to *regain* myths—they are being helped back into the world again. As Jung so often stated in so many different ways, *symbols* are a way of putting oneself in touch with the world— with external reality.

The other group of women who are outside the beauty myth are those who live by strongly ideological or religious values—i.e., nuns, Hassidic women, women in many traditional societies—and who have *other* symbols.

Glamour can only exist where women are no longer *morally* part of a symbolic universe, but belong to an a-moral technological consciousness which makes order of chaos.

Women everywhere, are placed on the side of chaos, disorder, the 'wild'. In Muslim societies, she is 'fitna' ('disorder, chaos' as well as 'beautiful woman'—the connotation of a femme fatale attraction which makes men lose their self control). Societies like the Muslim ones which segregate the sexes do so in order to contain woman's destructive, all-absorbing power. When she does enter a 'male space' she is veiled, 'invisible'. The street is such a space—a male space par excellence.

In our society woman's potentially destructive power is contained not by ritual and religious injunctions but by technological (and 'glamorous') ones. Whereas in Mediterranean and other societies, a man's *honour* is inextricably linked to a woman's purity and modesty, in our society a man's status—although independent of a female's 'purity'—is often linked to just how much a woman conforms to technological imperatives, like efficiency, problem-solving and measurability, which become part of her visible skin in the way she applies cosmetics, wears clothes and generally comports herself when, for example, the boss comes to dinner.

'Superwoman' in our society not only implies efficiency in housework, child-rearing and work, but a glamorous packaging on vital occasions such as dinner parties. Glamour brings women in from the Wild, onto the side of order, machines, manufacture and inevitably, myth.

CHAPTER 4

The Polluting Body

'Somewhere between the goddess and the demon is the menstruating woman . . .'

Paula Weideger, *Female Cycles*

The phenomenon of the polluting woman who, once monthly, is treated like 'a dangerous piece of radioactive material', to be secluded, shunned and deemed to possess 'witchy' qualities at menstruation and childbirth, has excited argument and anger among feminists, anthropologists and, more recently, poets alike.

The feminists, at one pole, regard all such taboos as 'female flesh-loathing'. Their argument is that this view of woman as 'dirt' keeps them in their lowly, servile position, reinforcing their economic and social exploitation. Purity laws, then, are seen as utterly degrading and negative, a male-chauvinist plot. Thus Adrienne Rich writes:

'Certainly, the menstrual cycle is yet another aspect of female experience which patriarchial thinking has turned inside out, rendering it sinister or disadvantageous.'

Germaine Greer would rather 'do without it', and so little understands symbolic values that she suggests woman taste their menstrual blood to prove their emancipation and carry their napkins openly to the loo. This would not prove emancipation but rather that the symbol of menstrual blood had lost its power to evoke anything at all, which is unlikely.

If the feminists suffer from too little symbolism, at the other pole there is a *surfeit* of symbols in the Jung, Eliade, Lévi-Strauss and recently, Penelope Shuttle-Peter Redgrove approaches to the subject, which see pagan symbols of rebirth everywhere, and tend to link women (and menstruation) to the moon. Lévi-Strauss, in a not too dissimilar fashion, relates the whole of culture to the fact of woman's menstruation and their *periodicity*. Time and the calendar are based on this periodicity, and men are concerned to retain this particular feature of women, which in turn has led then to subjugate them to 'regles' (which in French means both 'rules' and 'menstruation'). Enticing as these theories are, they are, in common with Freudian symbol analysis, not 'falsifiable', to use a Popperian criterion; neither are these interpretations in any way 'verifiable' in an objective sense except within the terms of their own system. In this sense such theories can hardly claim to be scientific. They afford at best a poetic, intuitive approach. A book like Shuttle-Redgrove's *The Wise Wound*, admirable though it is in many respects, leaves one wondering if a new best-seller might shortly appear in the bookstores entitled *Was God a Menstruating Woman*. Which is only to say that a Robert Graves-type enthusiasm has so carried away the two authors, and they now so *over*-evaluate menstruation and its hidden glories, that they succeed (or almost do) in finding evidence for it just about everywhere—from the film *The Exorcist* to the legend of the Holy Grail:

> 'The great non-Christian legend of the Middle Ages was that of the Quest of the Grail. The Christian Knights of King Arthur's Table were tormented by a vision of the cup used at the Last Supper that contained blood from the wounds of the crucified Jesus. Only the pure Knight without stain, Parsifal, was admitted into the Grail Castle, where the genitally maimed Fisher King sat awaiting the question that would bring life back into the Wasteland.

Parsifal watched the show of Knights and maidens carrying the lance dripping blood into the cup of the Grail,
and he was thunderstruck. He was speechless. Being speechless, he did not ask the question that would have redeemed
the Wasteland. He showed no curiosity. Thes how came
and went—and the Castle vanished. Parsifal had failed.

'The terrible fact is that the question was a very simple
one. It was "And whom does this Grail serve?" What is
this Grail, containing blood, for? It must now be obvious
to readers of this book what the meaning of *the Grail is in
a society that had forgotten its roots in feminine experience. The
Grail is the buried feminine secret* [my italics]. And the question
which nobody answers is, "Why does the woman bleed in
menstruation?" What is this cup full of blood for? That
"navel" full of wine? The Christian Knights tried to be
good without the feminine principle, yet the knowledge
of it came in this vision.'

And so on.

The inspiration for this interpretation came from the writings
of Jung's wife, Emma, who nonetheless treated the blood as a
'spiritualised symbol' without any concrete meaning on the
physical level.

In common with much of this kind of writing, the symbols
are taken totally out of context—both out of time and out of
place. One feels that the authors have failed to dissociate themselves from their own myth, and perhaps the book's most
remarkable feature is Peter Redgrove's involvement with
Penelope Shuttle's menstrual problems.

But to be fair, the book makes many valid points, too, not
least of which is the notion of psychic growth via the 'moment
of truth' of menstruation, though no doubt moments of truth
exist in illness, loss and trauma of all kinds. To select menstruation as the *unique* moment of truth is a gross distortion.
But like Von Daniken, and indeed generations of Kabbalists

before him, the authors try to prove a dominant motif by the skilful use of 'Gematria'[1]. This is not difficult, but the proof, in fact, constitutes no proof, for symbols and their interpretation are always arbitrary, depending on culture and context. Black, white, red are the dominant colours in symbolism (but they mean different things in different places). Sun and moon, likewise, appear everywhere.

In *Rethinking Symbolism*, Dan Sperber questions whether symbols can be said to have a meaning at all: '*If symbols had a meaning*,' he says, '*it would be obvious enough*' (my italics). What do they do then? Symbols can only be said to have *cognitive* and not *semiological* values: that is, they can only mean something to the person experiencing them. There is no *general* meaning. Symbols are never totally determined in their meaning. At most all they can do is focalize, evoke, and this 'evocation is never totally determined; there always remains to the individual a considerable degree of freedom; cultural symbolism focuses the attention of the members of a single society in the same direction, determines parallel evocational fields that are structured in the same way, but leaves the individual free to effect an evocation in them as he likes.'

Nonetheless symbols continue to hold great allure for the anthropologist. There is one systematic anthropological approach which attempts to place the symbols in a *total* system and to relate them to the society in question. Mary Douglas is one of the leading exponents of this kind of interpretation. She suggests in *Purity and Danger* that it is implausible to interpret such things as menstrual taboos as expressing something about the actual relation of the sexes, but that 'ideas about sexual dangers are better interpreted as symbols of the *relation between parts of society* [my emphasis] as mirroring designs of hierarchy or symmetry which apply in the larger social system. The two sexes can serve as a model for the collaboration and distinctive-

[1] Literally, the calculation of the numerical value of Hebrew words and the search for connections with other words and phrases of equal value.

ness of social units.' Believing passionately in man's need to live out his life with symbolic consonance, his inherent abhorrence of disorder and subsequent need for classification and boundary, Mary Douglas claims that all ideas about 'separating, purifying, demarcating and punishing trans- gressions, have as their main function to impose system on an inherently untidy experience'. She would have it that men- struation and its taboos are not to be considered in isolation just as menstruation, but as part of a wider system of pollution which includes mucus, sweat, excrement, childbirth, defilement etc. Looked upon in this light menstruation shrinks to just one more taboo, rather than expanding to the proportions of *The Wise Wound*. In her view, there is always danger lurking on the margins, in the transitional states. Menstrual blood does not quite fit any classification—she cites the Maoris who 'regard menstrual blood as a sort of human being manqué. If the blood had not flowed, it would have become a person, so it has the impossible status of a dead person that has never lived.' Menstrual blood, too, is thick and sticky—something between solid and liquid—that, too, adds to its lack of definition, its 'dangerous', unclassifiable quality.

One of the functions of pollution concepts is to enforce sexual role. Here, Douglas is on common ground with the feminists— but not for long, for she goes on to express the somewhat surprising notion that 'sex is likely to be pollution-free in a society where sexual roles are enforced directly', and gives the example of the Walbiri of central Australia:

'For the least complaint or neglect of duty Walbiri women are beaten or speared. No blood compensation can be claimed for a wife killed by her husband, and no one has the right to intervene between husband and wife. Public opinion never reproaches the man who has violently or even lethally asserted his authority over his wife. Thus it is impossible for a woman to play off one man against

> another . . . *These people have no beliefs concerning sex pollution. Even menstrual blood is not avoided, and there are no beliefs that contact with its brings danger'* [my emphasis].

She warns that 'when the principle of male dominance is applied to the ordering of social life but is contradicted by other principles such as that of female independence, or the inherent right of women as the weaker sex to be more protected from violence than men, then sex pollution is likely to flourish.'

What are we to make of this? What lessons can we learn from the sad fact of what Douglas calls the 'basic problem of wanting to have your cake and eat it?' In order to free themselves from menstrual taboos, do women have to resign themselves to violence?

Women in our society want to get rid of menstrual taboos altogether, but they also seek independence, and the right to be protected from violence. If the symbolic system of taboos is so interlinked with power structure; if to jettison the taboos means to invite direct violence (which is what I suspect is happening —witness the statistics of rape and battering) what solution is left to women? Must they revert to the seclusion of menstrual huts, and notions of curdling the milk? Perhaps one solution is to look at the whole phenomenon from a totally different angle. The writers discussed so far have approached menstrual taboos and their symbols from a non-cognitive point of view. While seeking out motifs, or structural relationships, it would perhaps be more profitable to ask. the women involved what these taboos mean to them. Do they in fact, as is so often suggested, feel degraded and inferior because of them, or do the rites of separation and re-integration give them anything positive of value?

While certain feminists make loud appeals for the 'reclamation' of menstruation, few would clamour for the retention of menstrual taboos which are generally viewed as an expression of men's hatred and envy of women and part of a systematic sexist plot. There is however, one very tiny ripple apparent among a very small minority of women—a move to recreate certain rites of separation and re-integration, which deserves noting.

Amongst Orthodox Jewish women in London, a despised lot by their liberated sisters, there has been quite a phenomenal increase in the number of 'mikvaoth' (ritual baths) over the past few years. Pre-war London had two 'mikvaoth' (Dunk Street and Essex Road). Today there are seventeen.[1] And this can be set against a context of religious decline in other Orthodox practices. How does one explain the growth in this one area assuming it is not simply a question of radical chic, ethnic chic or 'nouveau religiosity'? What possible appeal can the 'mikvah' have to an increasingly aware and secularised woman?

Orthodox Jewish women make Family Purity Laws (Tahar ath Hamishpaha), the laws regarding the separation of husband and wife for the 5 days during (niddah) and the 7 days following (tahara) menstruation, the cornerstone of their married life. During this time all physical contact is absolutely forbidden (and for this reason, Orthodox Jews are obliged to maintain twin-beds). At the end of the taboo period, the woman, stripped of everything including rings, totally immerses herself in the ritual bath and is then considered spiritually cleansed and renewed. If she does not use the 'mikvah' it is thought that her children and family could suffer from this ritual lapse. In this way it can be seen that Mary Douglas's thesis of purity laws as part of a wider system of control and beliefs seems to apply. Misfortunes of certain kinds can be blamed on a ritual lapse on the part of the woman who has allowed herself to remain dangerously unclean.

But what of this uncleanliness? How does the woman experience it? In our society where there is little *defined* men-

[1] I understand there has been a similar move among Zoroastrian women—a renewed interest in purification rites.

strual taboo—i.e., there is no definite purdah for women during menstruation, in fact very little recognition of menstruation altogether, it has been made invisible by tampons, the pill, etc.—but nonetheless a vague secrecy and shame attached to the subject, women tend to express the negative aspects of menstruation: it hurts, it's messy, it's associated with the horrors of pre-menstrual tension, or as it is sometimes called 'the premenstrual syndrome'—swellings, headaches, cramps, insomnia, kleptomania, irritability, mental illness, and in Germaine Greer's words:

> 'The fact is that no woman would menstruate if she did not have to. Why should women not resent an inconvenience which causes tension before, after and during; unpleasantness, odour, staining; which takes up anything from a seventh to a fifth of her adult life until the menopause . . . we would rather do without it.'

Paula Weideger in *Female Cycles* does not question that 'For a woman, the taboo acts as a constant confirmation of a negative self image. It represents the source of the shame she feels about her body and her sexuality.' This shows the extreme ethnocentric bias of a woman who can only talk from her own experience. Yet there are women in the world who actually *celebrate* menstruation and its taboos without making a Moon Goddess cult of it, and make it the cornerstone of their lives. The anthropologist Hildred Geertz told me of the *pride* she felt in being considered full of strange powers at the time of her menstruation in Bali, when she could not enter temples, etc. When I asked a group of Hassidic women in my field study what they felt about Purity Laws and ritual baths, there was not one who answered in a negative way. One saw it rather picturesquely as a 'hedge of roses'.[1] By this, she explained, she

---

[1] It is interesting that the same imagery applies in the Sleeping Beauty myth.

felt that they were a beautiful way of keeping the marriage partnership fresh and alive. 'No-one,' she said, 'could survive togetherness all the time. This way we have a break, and it's so much better when we get together again.' Another replied that you could only understand and appreciate the experience of the ritual bath when you did it. She felt renewed, refreshed —ready to start again. Similar responses were given by all the women. They all felt that modern life and particularly constant togetherness, caused a dulling of the marital relationship; they all felt, too, 'spring-cleaned' by the immersion, and most felt that women needed some time to themselves, a period of withdrawal. None expressed resentment at the 'pollution' aspects of the laws, but rather stressed the positive renewal values; they did, however, express dismay at the attitude of other, 'liberated' women who saw the laws as degrading and archaic, which they posited to their lack of experiential knowledge.

It would be facile to select these women's attitude toward purity laws, without referring to some of the other values in their society: marriage and child-bearing are highly valued— a woman has virtually no status until she is a mother; they practise little birth control; large families of between five to eight children are fairly common. In the particular group I studied, several women managed to work as well, but the arrival of a new child was always seen as a blessing. In the Kabbalistic universe they inhabit men and women each have a well-defined place; all things have a male and female aspect; but this seeming androgyny requires rigid physical separation of the sexes whose 'coupling' has cosmological implications. In Kabbalistic terms, when sexual union takes place in the world below—i.e., the earthly world—it is mirrored by a divine coupling in the heavenly spheres—the world above—which unites the male and female aspects of the Godhead. But there male and female aspects always remain distinct. Male and female relate but they never merge; the 'dynamic interplay of opposites' necessitates two opposing forces. Their world is determined by religious values which give a meaning to Death as well as to Life.

Blood as a symbol

Many writers view the menstrual taboo as a subcategory of the blood taboo—the idea that 'blood is life'. (Orthodox Jews for this reason ritually drain all the blood from meat before it is considered kosher.) By the same token one could postulate that blood is death. I remember my own horror and thoughts of imminent destruction some years ago, when, suffering from TB of the lungs, I coughed up blood with my sputum. It was a far more devastating and frightening experience than confronting one's menstrual blood. Blood 'out of place' inevitably arouses feelings of shock, extreme anxiety, and bodings of imminent disaster, as both men and women who have suffered sudden internal haemorrhaging will testify to.

Weideger uses the old evolutionary argument that 'the fear of blood is not a sufficient explanation . . . because the taboo has persisted into the present day when the horror of blood is no longer so great'. One could pertinently ask 'How does she know?' She automatically assumes a difference between 'Us' and 'Them' (the primitives) when much of contemporary anthropology points towards the exact opposite—that the mechanisms of the mind do not differ.

Some anthropologists have suggested the death association with anything amanating *from* the body, while, ingestion, or anything taken *into* the body on the other hand, is associated with nourishment and life. This leaves semen in an ambiguous position: emanating from the body, it is generally considered healthy, clean and life-giving. One account in *Female Cycles* stresses the positive value given to semen in oral sex while menstrual blood is rejected with distaste: 'His semen excites me. I swallow it and rub it on my face and breasts'; while her menstrual blood is nonetheless considered unclean. Jean La

Fontaine in *Perceiving Women* has commented that 'presumably semen is clean because of its fertilising qualities. It is not waste by definition, although it may be wasted.' Among the group of Hassidim I studied, semen was in fact considered as unclean and polluting as menstrual blood, and men had to take a ritual bath after every seminal emission, to purify themselves.

This leads us back to the question of what symbols *mean*, if they can be said to mean anything, or whether the only meaning is a *cognitive* one.

Some psychiatrists stress the relationship of our fear of menstrual blood to the 'birth-trauma' and our repression of it. Thus George Groddek holds that the menstrual cycle periodically reminds us of our birth experience by virtue of the fact that we subliminally smell blood each month, since blood was the first thing we smelt and tasted.

Blood, nonetheless, is the most powerful symbol of both life and death. Menstruation reminds us of both: but in a society where the woman cannot allow herself to give birth, and where Death, emptied of religious meaning, equals what Eliade has called 'Anguish before Nothingness', it is no wonder that menstruation and its taboos have been emptied of all meaning too and only the physiological, mechanistic shell remains, emerging as a frightening array of pre-menstrual or para-menstrual *symptoms*. Without religious values, menstruation can have no value either; at most a few ad hoc cults might be resurrected, but they, too, cannot be vested with any true meaning, as they will not be able truly to *relate the individual to the universe*.

One such cult is described by Paula Weideger in *Female Cycles* where she rightly considers menstruation in the same context as the menopause and female sexuality generally, but still limits her view to a 'sexual' one rather than a cosmological one. It recounts a long letter from a travelling lesbian commune in which the women recounted the individual experiences and menstrual histories of the members and described the pattern of menstrual synchrony that had evolved as they lived and travelled together. But the same feminist diatribe mars the otherwise valid suggestion that women attempt some kind of separatism when she suggests that lesbians can 'help hetero-sexual women to understand the extent to which fear of men's opinions and male power limits the search for self-knowledge'. Most women, however, do not live in communes of travelling lesbians, and their phenomenological stance is quite a different one. Most women would probably prefer to know how they could experience their menstruation to help them relate to men and the world generally.

But unless we can find a meaning in life and death generally, in a secular world we will find it hard to find anything but a biological place for menstruation in it (and, equally, the menopause). If the concept of re-birth has lost its meaning, so, too, must menstruation. The new cults (menstrual blood-tasting, placenta stew[1] and all) express *cultic* values rather than religious ones, and are of the same nature as fashionable yoga practices in the West. They do not, nor can they, provide a total symbolic consonance for the individual.

While on the one hand lauding the kind of puberty rites that Margaret Mead describes among the Arapesh, Weideger goes on to say that

> 'If such ceremonies existed in our culture, we would be campaigning to have them stopped. We would object to the practice and purpose of scarification, rubbing the genitals with nettles, and the emphasis on fertility. Our objections would be justified ,since these ceremonies per-petuate the taboo on menstruating women and narrowly define the role she is expected to play until the time when she comes to menopause.'

[1] Cooking and eating the placenta, 'fashionable' in some Californian communes (as reported in *The Birth Book*, Genesis Press).

While it is true that these ceremonies would not make sense in our society with its emphasis on birth control rather than fertility, Weideger has still underestimated their positive and cathartic symbolic action, in helping to smooth the girl's passage publicly from one life-stage to another. Women in our society have to make do with little symbolic action and consequently suffer a curious impoverishment, with just words left to take the place of ceremony and drama.

She places too literal a meaning on the taboo, too. The taboo is many things, not just a device to make women feel unclean—it is among other things a protective device, a device which safeguards cherished categories in the universe. I think, too, that she makes a mistake in equating our unease about menstruation with a full-fledged taboo. A taboo as such does not exist in our society; a conflict of feelings does, as it does with the subject of death. This conflict of feelings rather than a taboo exists because we have no religious or world view outside of the biological one in which to make sense of these feelings.

Perhaps the call to 'do away with menstruation' altogether is a logical consequence of this emptying of meaning; as, too, is, the call to do away with all menstrual taboos, whether implicit or explicit; for in our society, the taboo itself is an empty husk, a mere twitch, a cringe of discomfort, an embarrassment when we ask for tampons across the counter, an uncomfortable reminder that we cannot face death.

The women who take their monthly ritual bath are the fortunate ones. Eliade has spoken of the power of water, as 'formlessness', possessing 'this power of purifying, of regenerating, of giving new birth. Water purifies and regenerates because it nullifies the past and restores—even if only for a moment—the integrity of the dawn of things.' These women, too, have a period of quiet, almost of withdrawal from the world where they can listen to their bodies and use their 'moment of truth' as a springboard for the next time round, free from the shackles of togetherness imposed by the modern world.

The Shuttle-Redgrove book could be correct in its assertion that 'at the "moment of truth" of the paramenstruum, greater repressions may emerge, or may be expressed in body-language as illnesses or accident proneness'.

'SUPPOSE THAT SOCIETY IS A LIE, AND THE PERIOD IS THE MOMENT OF TRUTH WHICH WILL NOT SUSTAIN LIES.

' Thus a woman may with all goodwill and a desire for a peaceful life keep her feelings quiet about some dissatisfaction with her life, a bad habit of her lover's, some discrimination against her because she is a woman, or the necessity to study some subject which she is sure is irrelevant to her being. As a person conforming to society, she will for most of the month keep quiet about this, saying to herself, "it's all for the best . . . it's the principle of the thing . . . the greatest good for the greatest number". But then, maybe at the paramenstruum, the truth flares into her consciousness: this is an intolerable habit, she is discriminated against as a woman, she is forced to under-achieve if she wants love . . . In the absence of any significance given to her existence as a woman, then of course with each period these feelings may burst through!'

These feelings may burst through because they are given no other language in a society run by men, they cannot be expressed outwardly, so they screw women up inwardly.

It is not so much however that they cannot be given expression in a society '*run by men*', but that there is no ritual language available in secular society where religion has lost its hold. There are other societies run by men, such as the one I have described, where ritual forms exist precisely to give this 'moment of truth' expression.

What we have left of the menstrual taboo is little more than unease which leaves us to dwell on the physical ills: Hassidic women have a distinct ritual which gives them a common focus for sharing their experience, and powerful symbols for renewal. We are impoverished by our lack of ritual, but we cannot create it artificially, because, as Jung has said, 'symbols must live'—not only must they arise from the psyche, but they must have the power to connect the individual to the world, as it were. To do this they must be part of a wider system of meaning. There will no doubt be (and already is) a spate of new books on menstruation, and indeed every other aspect of woman's sexuality. A helpful new approach is one that uses the same techniques of body awareness and psychoprophylaxis as used to help women cope positively with childbirth. Thus through breathing, relaxation techniques and dietary supplements like Vitamin E, women can be relieved of or at least learn to accept some of the discomforts of menstruation. But this approach can only go so far, as can all the 'natural childbirth' approaches, as long as the body and its conditions continue to act as a potent metaphor for social change and social malaise. Everything from 'bat-mitzvahs' to 'witches' covens' have been suggested to help fill the ritual gap. But bits and pieces of ritual—ad hoc ritual—like the remnants of occult practices and Oriental religions that filter through into our society, can never provide for the same integration of the individual into the world as does a total systemic religion.

The demystification of women's bodies—the stripping away of myths and symbols—the reduction to mere flesh, bone and nerve-endings—finds a parallel expression in modern man's angst in the face of death. If there is no 'irreducible essence', as is claimed by those who wish to de-sex or de-mythologize, then life is indeed exactly how we see it, on a physical level only, nothing more; and Death is the great void. Could it be that the language of women's bodies is being used to express this bleak vision, and a new myth is thereby being created?

CHAPTER 5

The Birthing Body

'*Don't let them make you just another bolt in their great big tidy hospital clickity-clack machine. You are at the apex of alchemical force. Within your body another body has begun to move out to fulfil its destiny on earth. Get on with the miracle.*'

Danae Brook, *Naturebirth*

'*They want to have their babies in the middle of Hyde Park but if you can't do enough foetal heart monitoring, and the baby dies, they're likely to sue.*'

Midwife in *The Childbirth Book*, Christine Beels

'*We have emptied the notions of death and birth of everything not corresponding to mere physiological processes and rendered them unsuitable to convey other meaning.*'

C. Lévi-Strauss, *The Savage Mind*

The 'Battle of the Bulge' has been raging unabated now for over a decade. Childbirth has become the arena for the fight to the death between technology (modernization) and 'nature' (counter-modernization). Women are being armed ready for combat in various classes up and down the country; drilled to resist drugs, medical technicians, matron and machinery; conditioned to refuse enemas, pubic shaving, episiotomies and other medical rituals. They go into hospitals armed with handbooks, husbands, declarations of rights, and pots of honey. They learn battle cries of 'Home confinement', 'Bring back midwives' and 'No pethidin'. Never has there been such grassroots rebellion since the days of the Luddites, and we all know what fate awaited them! Women have not, as yet, exactly *smashed* monitoring devices, but this petticoat rebellion bears something of the same hallmark; the feeling that machinery has deprived man (woman) of something infinitely human and precious, and that, were it to be abolished, man could reclaim his birthright (or rather woman her right to give birth).

There is something, moreover, highly paradoxical in the fact that at the same time that childbirth is being increasingly medicalized, and 'active management of labour' promulgated as an ideal (labour, not, by the way, 'actively managed' by the mother, but by a team of technicians and machines), women are being encouraged and indeed *expecting* to think of labour and the act of childbirth as the greatest experiential 'high' of their lives. In Sheila Kitzinger's words, a matter of 'giving oneself mind and body to a creative experience in which, literally, love is made flesh'. Women are increasingly expecting to derive a *religious* experience from a physiological process, which logic and history tells us has been emptied of meaning by machinery, and worry enormously if the techniques they have learned to prepare them for this ecstasy in any way prove inadequate, and they do indeed have to reach for the pethidin.

A realistic look around, and the figures tell us that childbirth has never been more medicalized. Look, for example, at the changing figures of *home* versus *hospital* confinements. In 1946, half of the births in Great Britain took place at home. By 1958 the figure had fallen to 36 per cent; by 1970 to just over 12 per cent; and by 1978 to 3 per cent. In America home confinements have been almost totally phased out for some time.[1] Look too, at the figures for increasing surgical intervention in childbirth, and the rising popularity of the Caesarian section: In 1977, at least one out of every ten babies in the US was delivered surgically, and several hospitals in the UK show a startling increase in the number of Caesarians.

On the other hand, preparation for childbirth has increased correspondingly, with a mushrooming of ante-natal classes using various mixtures of psychoprophylactic or straight physiotherapy techniques, and although still largely aiming at the middle class, few women go into labour today without some expectation that they will have an easier time than their

---

[1] One could perhaps interpret the battle between hospital and home confinement as a reflection of the split between public and private spheres. In traditional societies no such division exists; all births are 'public' because the 'public' embraces everything.

mother or grandmother, and many have at least a tenuous knowledge of 'relaxation' and 'breathing', an acquaintance with the principles of Dick-Read or Erna Wright (if only through the Sunday papers), that they feel, hope, will equip them for all eventualities. Is it a question of 'Indian giving'? Are we giving women with one hand the hope and promise of an enriching experience, while with the other, immediately taking it all away? This was dramatically brought home to me when I taught psychoprophylaxis for a short while in a renowned London teaching hospital. On the one hand I was told to bolster the mothers' self-confidence by teaching them 'natural' techniques while at the same time recognizing that most would be on machines in any case. Many would come to my class saying 'I'm going to have an epidural or a Caesarian but I thought I'd learn the breathing anyway.' The women who had mastered the breathing would complain that they were all immobilized by monitoring devices anyway, while the anaesthetist who administered the epidurals complained the women 'couldn't push'. How many women today actually experience the 'high' promised them by the fortunate few? Ten per cent at one end of the scale experience childbirth as 'ecstatic', ten per cent the other end, as 'horrific', the rest are somewhere in between. Or have the promises themselves become a substitute for something else? Are women really being educated about their bodies, or has childbirth, like other life experiences, simply become the focus of a new cult? Whether it be the 'life-enhancing' one of the 'Naturebirth' advocates, or the mutilating one of the opposing Caesarian side?

The doctrines and influence of French obstetrician (though this seems too confined a word for him), Frederick Leboyer, well illustrate this new cult approach and its pitfalls.

Leboyer is a man of great charismatic persuasion (like his predecessor, Grantley Dick-Read), and the relationship of women to charisma as yet remains largely unexplored, though it is a commonplace of sociology that women are more prone to joining religious sects etc. Several writers have commented on the role of the gynaecologist as shaman. One is Paula Weideger in *Female Cycles*:

> 'In this culture, the gynaecologist functions as witch doctor ... the gynaecologist has taken upon himself the role of diviner. He assesses the quality of normal female behaviour —normal not only in the biological sense but in a social sense as well. By his own declarations he has specialized knowledge of a woman's body, her real spiritual potential, and the true nature of her unconscious mind. ...
>
> 'The shaman believes that he is apart from the culture and in a transcendent state of communication with the gods; ... The gynaecologist is "more royal than the King". ...'

Then she says, 'If the magical system is to work (the object of the magic) must support it.' In her opinion our acceptance of it stems from the fact of our 'shameful feelings about menstruation and menopause' and our acceptance of the taboo. And 'How are we going successfully to change the relationship between women and the gynaecologist?' While sharing the problems with other women helps to some extent it is no real answer. The first steps she suggests (taken from Virginia Woolf) are 'ridicule' and 'laughter'.

Another commentator is Sheila Kitzinger:

> 'The obstetrician, as distinct from the midwife who is traditionally far less interventionist, seeks to take control of childbirth. It is then almost as if he, and not the woman gives birth to the baby. The intricate technology has defused the bomb, childbirth has been de-sexed. The previously mysterious power has been analysed, and he has harnessed it to a masculine purpose and according to a masculine design.'

The priests then, of the new church of technology, are men. Childbirth, previously an art, has been turned into a science. But back to Leboyer. The French doctor and several writers have commented on the role of gynaecologist as shaman, and at first glance he seems to embrace the counter-modernity movement, with his 'naissance avec tendresse' approach, his stress on a massage for newborns, derived from the Indian sub-continent, and the veto on such features of modernity as electric lights. At second glance, however, we can see he and his cult could only be a modern invention, in the same league as countless other charismatic sect leaders, and certainly if 'nature' had intended a newly-born babe to have had a warm bath on birth, it would have provided one *on* or *in* the mother's body—but it doesn't—so how can Dr Leboyer know that this is precisely what the new born needs? No, his bath, if not needed by 'nature', is needed 'ritually' in order not only to make the babe's passage from womb to world, but to legitimize the shaman's own authority.

Sheila Kitzinger, rightly indignant, wrote an article in *The Times*, July 27, 1977, condemning some of the more *outré* Leboyer practices, and the way they further sapped the mother's confidence. Commenting on his rules of silence at delivery she writes:

'Why should the mother's spontaneous cries at the climax of delivery be curbed because someone else believes that babies should be delivered into silence?

'I believe that the mother's natural reactions are the right ones and that every baby should be welcomed by human voices . . .

'It is women who bear the babies. Perhaps it is time for women to say exactly what they would like in labour and at birth. No cult should get in the way of a mother's first-hand experience of the baby she has just pushed out into the world. This can apply as much to the cult of the

ritual bath as to the technological cult of hospital birth in
what all too often looks like a well-equipped torture
theatre.'

Leboyer has also suggested the introduction of a cell
'sauvage' within the hospital—a squatting space—where the
mother would be free to do her own thing—but notice, it is
within the hospital, not in Hyde Park, the forest or even the
mother's own home. There are two elements in this which bear
commenting upon. The first is Peter Berger's 'law' that '*Almost
any contact between different cognitive systems leads to mutual contamination*'. With Leboyer and his cult, we definitely see two
systems at work—hospital (i.e., Culture) and nature. 'Mutual
contamination' may not be everyone's way of describing the
resulting mix, but no doubt next door to the cell 'sauvage'
will be a room full of monitoring devices.

The second point relates to the ritual effectiveness of keeping
the hospital as the arena for all the magic. With all the best will
in the world, the room scrubbed up at home with Dettol still
lacks ritual panache, however many white sheets are put down.
This is why the majority of women would still opt for the
hospital for labour, in spite of the reassuring figures from
Holland produced by the protagonists of home confinement.

Women, then, are exposed to at least three forces when con-
fronted with childbirth: technology, nature and magic (charisma, cult, ritual or whatever).

Like all successful contemporary religious leaders, Leboyer
selects his symbols, some old, some new, and manipulates them:
massage and bathing, two symbols we find again and again in
religious cults; low lights and low voices merely add to the
mystique. To pretend that they are all for the benefit of the
newborn is absurd and unproveable, but this is not to deny
that to some they bring some additional meaning and enrichment to a situation in which the birth otherwise would be
reduced to a 'physiological husk'. For Leboyer to become a

religion rather than a cult he would have to evolve a complex
'life' schema, relating birth to the total unfolding and finally,
death, of the individual child. Birth, like menstruation, or
indeed, like its opposite, death, suffers from a lack of religious
or ideological framework. It has become almost impossible for
a woman to make sense of it as an experience without this
over-arching framework, so she has latched on to bits and
pieces from everywhere, clutching at psycho-sexual theory
here, Leboyer there, and body awareness somewhere else, and
finally her surrender to the needle or the knife with a bit of
gymnastics thrown in. 'Bricolage'[1] in the true sense.

There are some societies where the 'new' approaches seem
to work; where there is such overall consensus as to the values
of that society, one 'method' can work. Take, for example,
Sheila Kitzinger's account of childbirth in East Germany:

> 'Exercise classes take place in a gymnasium . . . and are
> led by a gymnast. The emphasis is upon muscle training
> and athleticism: "Breathe in 1 2 3 4. Breathe out 1 2 3 4 5 6:
> Breathe in. Breathe out. Relax." The commands are
> rapped out like a drill sergeant.'

Note that, unlike our society, 'the instructress is not concerned with the mother's subjective sensations—only with her
correct behaviour. The discipline of psycho-prophylaxis is used
as a means by which the pregnant and labouring woman is
assimilated to Communist values and her behaviour regulated.'
Since we have few agreed-upon values to which to assimilate
our mothers, psycho-prophylaxis cannot work in the same way.
Far from wishing to impose one set of values, we clamour for
choice and more choice. 'A woman must have choice' has
become the slogan of our age, and paradoxically, this only
serves to compound the existing fragmentation.

---

[1] Picking out bits and pieces of culture from everywhere and combining them in
new patterns, rather like a patchwork quilt.

The increasing participation of fathers (itself somewhat ironic in an era when marriage has never been more shaky, and this year's feller is likely to be next year's fade-out) exhibits a similar desperation. As Mary Douglas writes in *Implicit Meanings*:

'It would be worth looking for a correlation between practice of the couvade, weak definition of marriage, and a strong interest in the husband's part in asserting his claim to the wife and her child. In England we might expect the couvade to be found in sectors of society where the husband is forced to be absent for long periods from home; in tribal society where the marriage tie is weak. The couvading[1] husband is saying "Look at me, having cramps and contractions even more than she! Doesn't this prove I am the father of her child?" It is a primitive proof of paternity . . . Already one notices a new emphasis on the father's role in the lying-in of the mother, and a new responsibility for the mental health of his children, an emphasis which I would expect to be increasing with the greater ease of divorce.'

The cult of couples (some hospitals and classes despotically insist that a woman can only come to a class if she brings her mate) has rapidly caught on in this country; husband-coached labours are, in some circles, considered ideal, and many women feel pressurized into bringing their husband to childbirth classes and indeed, insisting on his presence at the birth, even when very little in their relationship warrants this kind of intimacy. While the majority of husbands do offer a good deal of support to their wives, for a minority, the presence of the husband is positively counter-productive, and indeed, I have a growing feeling (from my own experience of teaching

[1] The common practice of the husband 'going into labour' at the time of his wife's confinement.

'couples') that an increasing number of women would actually prefer their husbands not to be there at all. But cult pressure is so strong at this particular time that it would be heresy even to hint at this. For a man, suddenly to be flung into the barriers-down situation of birth can prove shattering; contrary to popular myth, it does not cement husband and wife together for the rest of their lives (as a cursory glance at divorce figures will show). The idea that it is a shared labour can be misleading, too, for the feelings, the pain, the agony or the ecstasy can only be individual and private in the final analysis. The act of giving birth is always unique to each woman—what she can share are only the externals—inside she is alone as with all pain's bodily sensations. The husband either comes to treat his wife like a behaviorist puppet, 'measuring' contractions, 'applying' this or that technique, 'conducting' her labour with commands and exhortations; or, properly appreciating that this is an experience from which, by definition, he is excluded, is seized by jealousy and resentment, which may explode at some later date. 'The man should not forget that however sophisticated the machinery, it is she who is having the baby.' Many men do forget however, and take over in ante-natal classes.

The exclusion of men from labour traditionally served to protect both men and women from the rawness of their feelings. It allowed women to express themselves free from the tie of togetherness. Today, the woman not only has to worry about how she performs in labour, vis-à-vis her ante-natal teacher and the hospital staff, but also vis-à-vis her husband or boyfriend. One mother of my acquaintance went into labour in full wig, false eyelashes and film make-up so that she looked good on her husband's home movie of the birth later on!

The participation of men in childbirth today also reflects their increasing uncertainty and anxiety about their role in life. No longer patriarchal heads of families with clearly defined roles, they nonetheless feel that they have to participate in some way in this their wife's event in order to be part of the whole. The eagerness with which most men have seized upon the opportunity to take part in the birth speaks as much of their identity crisis as anything else. Men, no longer sure of their place in the scheme of things, clutch at any opportunity to do their bit. Their identity crisis, in turn can engender a similar one in the wife. ('I felt he was jealous of my breast-feeding' is becoming a fairly common complaint. One father even asked me if there was any way in which he could produce milk to enable him to breast feed.) The new emphasis on dads is part of a society where the father's role has been as devalued as the mother's, and ad hoc solutions are being suggested to salvage identities.

Like, 'bonding', the all-important first few minutes, when throughout the animal world, a relationship is established between mother and child, 'couples' have been seen as a palliative to cure women's—or indeed, the whole of society's—ills. Thus it is suggested, that 'couples' participation promotes stronger husband-wife ties, i.e., stronger marriage, more intense parent-child relationship, etc. There is as yet little evidence to support this claim, although there is little doubt that the husband has been called upon to fill the gap, and provide the support usually supplied by a network of supportive others (relatives). This is proving too much for him and having the opposite of the desired effect.

Similarly, bonding has become the magic panacea, guaranteed to build a better world. Bonding in the animal world is simply a practical way of ensuring that the young are taken care of: no more, no less. But we have imposed our heavily subjective viewpoint on the whole matter. Although no-one would wish to deny the importance and indeed desirability of bonding, are we then able to say, with certainty, that, given that 'bonding' has taken place in those first few minutes, it will guarantee a lifetime of trouble-free, loving relationships, a better person, a more balanced individual, a more creative person? Or conversely, are we categorically able to state that the unfortunate individual whose mother was flat out on his arrival, has thereby been doomed to a life of crime, disruption and mental illness? Although it is true that bonding must facilitate the mother-child relationship in the early days, what she does from then on in can depend on a multitude of factors. There is no evidence to show that adoptive mothers, for example, are not as capable of providing tender loving care for their children.

Yet so easy is it to be seduced by reductionist thought, that there are those who would reduce all of life, or the ability of the individual to cope with life, to those two minutes after birth, just as there are those who would reduce the husband-wife relationship to a question of whether or not the man had been present at the birth or had joined in his wife's ante-natal classes. It is comforting indeed, to be able to reduce life to a mere five minutes or half an hour. There has, of late, been a noticeable proliferation of 'birthing' cults—'Primal Scream therapy' is a popular variant—with even Ronald Laing, with a total shift of emphasis in his writing recently, lending support to their theories. He has enthusiastically espoused Leboyer and his cause, and this leads one to wonder if he will shortly revise all his earlier theorising.

Modern childbirth, then, like technology itself, has a Utopian quality: it promises to deliver us, through either the use of the right techniques, or the right machinery (and sometimes a combination of both), or even by adopting the 'right attitudes' towards such things as 'couples' or 'bonding', from all of life's later vicissitudes. Never has anything held out such promise, and rarely has anything brought such disappointment.

The let-down usually does not happen immediately: it takes a while for the Utopian glow to wear off, and to be replaced by the growing realization that life after all is more complex than the ante-natal books promised; that in spite of a beautiful birth, you still hate your mother-in-law and feel resentful that your husband didn't get that rise, and wish you lived in a detached house, and had better legs.

In other societies, birth is not made a 'thing in itself'. Nor, contrary again to popular myth, is it necessarily less painful. Nancy Fuller and Brigette Jordan, working among mothers and midwives in Yucatan (Central America) in 1973, came to the conclusion that 'there is nothing to support the widespread myth that "primitive" childbirth is any easier than a "civilized" delivery.' The differences lay more in the mother's *expectations* (pain here was regarded as an inevitable part of having a child) and to some extent in the social support she received (noticeably from *women* only—mother, in-laws, sisters and friends, who bullied and harangued her, as well as reached out to her body lying across a wide hammock).

The effects of technology, or the 'medicalization of life' has been both to provide reliable birth control and significantly to lower the infant mortality rate. This means that not only can the mother choose to have her child *when* she wants but that she will be safe to assume it will survive. This in turn means that she will have a greater sense of 'futurity' than women previously had; she can look ahead to afterwards; invest in the child, plan for him, think ahead in terms of her own life. Childbirth becomes part of the life-planning of a rational, functional, technological society. Sheila Kitzinger, in *Women as Mothers*, writes of the middle-class women who regard child-bearing as 'an interruption of their "real lives" ' and goes on to say that, 'because they intend to have only one or two babies these women may feel that it is very important that they perform perfectly'. ('They' being both mother and child.) A woman who had no idea when her next child would come along, and could therefore have few thoughts about going back to work or re-training for the 'real world', correspondingly felt little need for an experiential 'high' at each point. The very notion of a 'real' world and an 'unreal' world is a modern one—a function of technological consciousness.

Peter Berger talks of the emergence of 'double consciousness', the 'componentiality' of the self, which is very relevant to women and the way they perceive their identity crises:

'The componentiality of the cognitive style pertaining to technological production extends to identity. ... A specific kind of double consciousness develops. In this case the dichotomy is between concrete identity and anonymous identity. The individual now becomes capable of experiencing *himself* in a double way: as a unique individual rich in concrete qualities *and* as an anonymous functionary. This dichotomization in the subjective experience of identity makes it possible for the individual to establish subjective distance vis à vis certain features of this identity.

'For example, the individual will now experience that portion of his identity that contains his anonymization as a "worker" as being "less real" than his identity as a private person or family man. Since each portion of identity relates to specific roles, it now becomes possible for the individual to perform some of these roles "tongue in cheek". The componentiality of identity, as the componentiality of social relations, makes possible an "engineering" practice. This time what is involved is the "engineering" of one's own self. Those aspects of identity that are defined as "more real" must be protected against threats coming from the "less real" components of identity. Very importantly, a psychological management of considerable complexity is necessary in order to perform actions "tongue in cheek". This is a precarious business— effort consuming, requiring a lot of thought and intrinsically unstable. In extreme cases the individual in this situation will experience "alienation", that is, he will no longer be able to recognise himself in this *or* the other component of his subjective identity. In the common usage of the notion of alienation only one type of such non-recognition has been stressed: the case where the individual can no longer recongize himself in this *anonymized identity*. *It is important to stress that the other type is just as possible, that is, the individual may feel alienated from precisely those components of his self that are not anonymized. While the individual may seek psychological refuge from the alienations of his work situation in private life, it is also possible that an individual may seek such refuge in the very anonymity of his work situation because he finds the non-anonymous relations of private life intolerable* [my emphasis].

The latter situation seems to be the one that many women find themselves in, with their 'work' identity more real than their 'home' one, while for many men, though not all, it seems to be the other way round.

All of which leads us back to the question of *choice* and modern consciousness.

'Nothing could be more modern than the idea that Man has a choice between different paths of social development,' Berger goes on, 'One of the most pervasive characteristics of traditional societies is the notion that there is no choice; that the structures of the given society are inevitable, rooted in human nature, or indee in the very constitution of the cosmos.'

Women in our society feel a split between their world and the so-called other world, because they are offered choices; they can decide to have or not to have a child; to have that child in hospital with full medical technology, at home 'naturally' or (decreasingly, but it is still possible in theory) opt for a combination of the two; they can choose to breast or bottle feed; can be full-time mothers, part-time mothers, or go back to work and leave the baby in someone else's care. They can follow Freud, Montessori, Spock or their own mothers; they can bring the child up with or without formal religion, or with disparate elements from several; they can eat vegetarian, macrobiotic or regular diets, fresh, frozen or canned foods; choose between several forms of birth control or none at all; choose the techniques they will use in love-making; choose make-up, fashions or hair-styles. And as the choices multiply, so does the fragmentation. How can a woman avoid feeling that somewhere out there is a 'real world', a world of 'wholeness', whether it be in an office, school, factory or university, more real than the world of the household, when she is forced to live in so many different worlds and faced with unending choices. The concept of 'real life' could only exist in a world where alternative life-worlds are conceivable. It is paradoxical that at one pole we find woman the acted upon, woman of no choice, woman the exploited, whereas at the other we find woman who is called upon to make constant choices. It is the same pole that sees the process of modernization as both redemption and damnation.

Technology, which imposes such an all pervasive consciousness, also seems to offer us choices; technology, however, or technological consciousness, always wins. 'Mechanized culture has led to mechanized birth', but it has also, ironically, given us the freedom to choose alternative ways.

The mother who has done battle for her home confinement will also make sure that she has an emergency 'Flying Squad' on hand, just as the most fanatical Naturopaths will still agree to a shot of penicillin in the case of pneumonia. The few exceptions to this—the few people who act consistently, like the religious sect in the recent case in Holland who refused polio vaccination and thereby sparked off a new epidemic of polio, or the Christian Scientists who reject transfusion—hit the headlines, precisely because they are so rare. Most of us only fight half-hearted battles, for deeply entrenched in us all is the promise that technology holds out of deliverance from suffering, even death.

Technology has its own enticing quality; its own allure. Who would not be dazzled by the following, quoted from Sheila Kitzinger's *Women as Mothers*?

> 'Abdominal girth, position of the fetus, haemoglobin counts and other blood tests, urine tests for sugar protein, other tests of blood or urine for oestriol production from the placenta, pelvic assessment, abdominal and vaginal examinations, sonar scans and perhaps an amniocentesis to detect whether or not the foetus has a chromosome abnormality or spina bifida or microcephaly or . . . there seems to be no end to the fascinating investigations which can be made.'

We overlook the fact that science does not always keep its promises—that more handicapped babies are being born each year, some as a direct result of 'improved' medical techniques, for medicine promises that with its aid, we will all give birth to live, healthy babies. Even the oft-quoted figures from Holland, where half of all births take place at home and which has the third lowest maternal mortality rate in Europe, fail to convince us that the lowered infant mortality (20 per thousand births) is not a direct product of medical intervention, but rather due to an improved standard of living all round. Like all ideologies, trying to attract new recruits, science offers you the horror stories first and then says, 'You will be saved 'if'' only unlike religion it provides no way of coping with suffering and injustice—no theodicy, its rites although they exist are inadequate. In fact we feel cheated by them rather than renewed.

There is a recent observable trend to include the teaching of 'stillbirth' and 'handicap' in ante-natal classes; this reflects the desperate lack of ideological framework for 'birth'. What does it say about our society that we now have to hold classes in 'Death'—enlightenment or loss? Are we trying to replace lost rites by group discussion and workshops? Can we create shared meanings through these classes, or do they further contribute to emptying death of all meaning?

Whatever this new awareness of death does, it would be facile to think of it as providing a real framework for human suffering. Like Encounter groups of all kinds it can afford temporary relief and an arena for psychodrama, but it would be misleading again to see it as more than an ad hoc solution filling a gap created by lack of meaningful ritual.

When Van Gennep coined the phrase 'rites de passage' he had in mind several things: a rite de passage smoothed the transition for the individual from one ritual state—one life passage—to another. A rite de passage also helped the whole community accept the change in that individual from one state to another.

A rite de passage neutralized the rather dangerous power that someone 'in between states' possessed—for society does not like 'betwixt and between' states. Finally, a rite de passage stamped, as it were, the culture on the individual.

The individual, by donning white wedding dress, black mourning garb or whatever, symbolized his state: society separated him for a while, and then brought him back in with appropriate ceremony which focused everyone's mind and emotions on the changes taking place and on the specific values of that society. Technological society has its own rites de passage for childbirth, whether they include ante-natal examinations, admission procedures, the donning of white gowns, and the 'ritual' purging of the enema. Women, however, are rebelling against their passive immobile roles in these, when they are 'ground down to be fashioned anew'. Victor Turner, the anthropologist, writes thus of all 'neophytes' whether in the bush or in modern hospitals:

'The passivity of neophytes to their instructors, their malleability, which is increased by submission to ordeal, their reduction to a uniform condition, are signs of the process whereby they are ground down to be fashioned anew and endowed with additional powers to cope with their new station in life.'

The other side, the 'naturebirth' side, has come up with new rites, whether they consist of rigorous gymnastics or Leboyer massage, Adele Davis diets or Yoga for childbirth: new symbols have been found. But because we still live in a fragmented society (a plural society) they are doomed to failure (or only moderate success). At the moment, women are in a state of confusion, for the necessary transformation of consciousness which would have to be effected in order for the new symbols to work, has not really taken place. We still basically believe in technology. It is too hard to dislodge from our consciousness, but we cannot accept the fragmentation it brings with it. Childbirth has become the battlefield for a new Holy War: we have yet to see if either side can bring about anything but a stalemate.

CHAPTER 6

The Ageing Body

'*Is it not strange that desire should so many years outlive performances.*'

Shakespeare

'*In a changing world, where machines have a very short run of life, men must not be used too long. Everyone over fifty-five should be scrapped.*'

Edmund Leach, 1968

'*The natural processes of corruption and decay have become as disgusting as the natural processes of birth and copulation were a century ago.*'

Geoffrey Gorer, *Death, Grief and Mourning in Contemporary Britain*

Our attitude toward the ageing body, both male and female, has been profoundly influenced by two things. The first is the machine paradigm of the body and the idea that the old and less efficient apparatus must be scrapped and replaced with a new and more efficient one. The second is the decline of orthodox religious beliefs concerning an after-life. The combination of these two things means that the ageing body is looked upon, in our society, with a mixture of horror and despair, reflected in our attitudes towards ageing generally, with the elderly losing status as they approach old age, waiting like used engines to be shunted off to the end of the line, rather than the reverse as in traditional societies. There the elderly receive increased responsibility and status, and with a new body of myth which actively seeks to deny the whole process of ageing and, by implication, death itself. Although both men and women fall prey to these 'swindles' (wigs, cosmetics, silicones and pollyannaish attitudes) in Alex Comfort's words, the main focus of this chapter will be on two current myths for women. One involves a whole drug industry in the guise of Hormone Replacement Therapy, which tells us that we can remain 'Feminine Forever' .The other promises the older woman unlimited sexual freedom and partners. Both draw heavily on the stereotype of the older woman as witch—a stereotype which is far from dead in our society.

Since the '60s, the menopausal woman has received much attention; whether or not the drug industry itself was responsible for a massive 'swindle', as some recent reports have suggested, is almost beside the point: the medical model of ageing is so entrenched that if it hadn't been hormones, no doubt something else would have been hailed as the new elixir. Not only does recent research demolish the whole notion of 'hormone reductionism', it also suggests that the 'menopause' itself may be of much wider implication, not specifically female. Thus in their book *The Male Menopause*, Derek Bowskill and Anthea Linacre examine the 'myth' of male menopause:

> 'The "male" menopause may be a dreamy sleep for some, but for others it is a terrible nightmare; harbinger of the autumn of an unlived life . . . the great disposer . . . In the past, and in many cultures even today, a man could rely on age to bring him some respect. Even if he had gained little esteem during his early years and had done little to deserve or justify even the smallest bubble of reputation, he could rest assured that middle age would earn him some respite from stress and strain and he would reap the minimum reward of his society accepting that he would "grow wiser and better as my strength wears away". Times have changed . . . What were once the virtues and worthwhile tributes and attributes of middle age no longer stand as consolations for the fear or grief of a possibly waning virility.'

Then there is the psychiatrist, Dr Michael Bott, quoted as saying:

> 'It seems sensible to look at the menopause syndrome as an entity—*affecting both men and women and having probably similar causation in both sexes* [my emphasis]. I would

describe what occurs as involutional melancholia—
corresponding to the depression that sets in with people
who come unstuck with the menopause',

and then, later on, on the subject of hormones:

'It's too easy to suggest that hormonal changes are responsible for this mid-life crisis—especially the impotence.
It's surprising how rarely one finds that impotent males
have any disturbance of their hormonal levels, and I know
of no research that suggests that it is the case with the
male menopause.'

Thus a more proper way of considering the menopause and
its symptoms would be in terms of ageing generally and the
values that society places on that process; the most important
element being the way that society views death. Simone de
Beauvoir in *Old Age* emphasises 'meaning' and old age:

'The meaning or the lack of meaning that old age takes
on, in any given society, puts that whole society to the
test, since it is this that reveals the meaning or the lack
of meaning of the entirety of the life leading to that old
age ... It is the meaning that men attribute to their life;
it is their entire system of values that define the meaning
and the value of old age.'

As Illich has said:

'In every society the dominant image of death determines
the prevalent concept of health.'

Furthermore, views on death are intricately related to what
happens *after* death; in our society, there is very little defined
belief about the future life and so we live with the fantasy that

physical decomposition and death can be warded off, given the right 'tinkering', 'spare parts' surgery, dietary supplements or hormone replacement therapy.

We have succeeded in making old age itself a disease, and this is nowhere more evident than in the mythology regarding the menopausal woman.

In the mid 1960s a book appeared which did much to open up the subject of the menopausal woman and to promote the widespread use of hormone replacement thereapy—Robert A. Wilson's *Feminine Forever*. Here, in the guise of 'gallant Knight' coming to the rescue of the fair lady in her 'despairing years', Wilson painted a most repellent picture of the ageing woman. Referring to the menopause as 'castration' (surely an example of the most obvious male-type projection ever), he gives an inventory of menopausal symptoms that would qualify most 50-year-old women for the Chamber of Horrors. They include dry tissues, weak muscles, sagging skin, brittle porous bones, dowager's hump, flabby withered breasts, stiff unyielding vaginas, cracked inflamed skin, as well as the well-known hot flushes, chronic indigestion, back-ache, and a host of other complaints ranging from dizziness to memory loss. Amongst the 'shrunken hags' he describes, we hear of 'untreated women who had shrivelled into caricatures of their former selves', some even turning into dwarfs 'due to pathological bone changes caused by lack of estrogen'. His imagery throughout, heavily dependent upon adjective and simile, is remarkable for its nightmare quality; at times one could almost be reading Grimm's fairy-tales. We have the 'witches' on the one hand— i.e., women who age naturally—and on the other those blessed by the fairy-godmother (hormones) with Eternal Youth; for those who have had the good fortune to receive oestrogen treatment 'at fifty . . . look thirty' and at 60 'looks and acts like forty' (he does not say what happens at 80). He gives the impression that the clock could be put back indefinitely, and the 'feminine forever' now prance around on the tennis courts with plumped-up skin and bosoms, looking wonderful in their tennis dresses, finding 'growth and enrichment of woman-hood', equipped for an 'enduringly feminine role in modern life', while the 'untreated', 'castrated' old hags huddle together with their blue rinses and brittle bones in delicatessens through-out the US with laughs, the author seriously tells us, resembling 'malicious cackles':

> 'Such women generally flock together in small groups of three or four. Not that they have anything to share but their boredom and trivial gossip. Clustering together in monotonous gregariousness they hide themselves from the rest of the world. They go together to the same hair-dresser to have their hair tinted purple as though they were schoolgirls again. They dress alike, buy the same little hats, and hobble slowly to the delicatessen shop to buy day after day, the same cold roast beef and potato salad; for they have long ago resigned from the more challenging responsibilities of their kitchens. Typically such women have no trace of humour. Spontaneous laughter is unknown to them, though they are capable of a kind of malicious cackle.'

It is not hard to see the 'witchy' characteristics the author has projected onto these unfortunate older women. The choice of language alone reeks of the childhood nightmare. This fairy-tale, this morality fable, was written more than a decade ago, when women perhaps did indeed believe that her 'body was the key to her fate', and that 'social and psychological fulfil-ment' all depended on one crucial test: 'her ability to attract a suitable male and hold his interest over many years'. But Women's Lib hasn't changed that much (although it has, to some extent, taken issue with the hard-sell of hormones), and numerous clinics are in operation today with the sole purpose of administering hormone therapy. As it turned out, the scientific evidence surrounding the mythology was highly debatable. Firstly, we don't know what 'causes' the menopause. Secondly, we don't know if hormones really make any difference one way or another, and thirdly, further confusing the issue, are the cancer implications; one side can produce evidence that oestrogen actually *reduces* cancer, while the other can produce evidence to support its claim, that it actually promotes cancer.

Paula Weideger in her book *Female Cycles* gives a fairly detailed account of the research done on the possible link between endometrial cancer and the use of Estrogen Replacement Therapy, and concludes that

> 'it is shocking and angering that years after animal experiments yielded results that indicated a connection between oestrogen and breast cancer, years after oestrogen therapy was widely introduced as a means of lessening the distress of menopause, and years after millions of women began taking this therapy, the first long-range studies on its effects are just being published. And, in the case of breast cancer, the results are alarming *and* inconclusive.'

She cites among others the suggestive but inconclusive findings of the Robert Hoover trials (see Robert Hoover, Laman A. Gray, Philip Cole and Brian MacMahon, 'Menopausal Estrogen and Breast Cancer', *New England Journal of Medicine*, August 1976). The study done by J. C. Bruch, B. F. Byrd Jr., and W. K. Vaugh, investigating the long-term effects of ERT on a group of 737 women who had hysterectomies shows that they had about the same incidence of breast cancer as other women in the general population, and a *lower incidence* of other cancers than predicted for the general population of postmenopausal women, and concludes: 'The most striking finding in this group is the unexpectedly low mortality rate from all causes.' Whereas Hoover's study tells us that ERT may cause breast cancer or at least stimulate its development.

As Weideger comments, 'In both cases the experiments are weak . . . At the moment, we do not know which set of results is the more reliable.' And the controversy continues to rage.

Explanation of menopausal symptoms include the 'hormone deprivation theory', which leads to the concept that for a third of a woman's life cycle, her body is malfunctioning; the 'rate theory', which posits that it is the rate at which oestrogen production declines that is crucial, but which can almost instantly be refuted on the grounds that women *under* thirty who have surgically induced menopause do not seem to suffer post-operative symptoms, although there is a sharp decline in oestrogen. And finally there is the 'addiction' theory (which is fast overtaking even the virus theory as an all-purpose theory —used to explain anything from obesity to allergy), which claims that menopausal symptoms are withdrawal symptoms. None of these theories can explain however, why some women (only 10 per cent in our society) suffer no menopausal symptoms or why some women fail to respond at all or only minimally to oestrogen.

Depression, for example, is often treated as a menopausal symptom, but in a recent paper[1] S. Ballinger made the point that whereas oestrogen is usually administered to treat depression in the menopausal woman, it is in fact *the depression that causes the oestrogen level to drop in the first place.* Hormones and their functioning are by no means a one-way process. Every woman knows, for example, that one very sure way to boost her oestrogen level, and thus improve her skin and hair, is to fall in love. Could this, by the way, be one of the reasons why Los Viejos of the famed Vilcabamba of Ecuador live so long and so healthily? Grace Halsell has described this community of centenarians where the custom is 'love at any age',

[1] See bibliography.

and she herself had to fight off the attentions of one ardent hundred-year-old!

Love, esteem and status must all have a marked effect on hormone levels, and possibly this is why one psychiatrist reported never having seen a menopausal psychosis in Chinese women. This she attributed to the fact that in China the older woman has a secure and coveted position. Oestrogen, then, goes some of the way, but not all the way, to explaining why some women can live happily with approaching age and others cannot. The 'Feminine Forever' myth brought menopause out of the closet, as it were, and even in the midst of repudiation generated other myths. There is a growing emphasis on the reclamation of the menopause, a cry for it to be treated as a 'natural' rather than 'medical' event (e.g., Weideger: 'If large numbers of menopausal women come to believe that menopause is a natural process, a more satisfactory method of responding to women's needs will be created'), an effort to convert its negative values to positive ones, calling for consciousness-raising and the like among menopausal women. Weideger in *Female Cycles* again:

'It is time for women to reclaim menstruation and menopause. Each day one of these cycles is part of our lives; yet we live with a male idea of how we ought to feel about them. We may clasp the earth mother to our breasts and proclaim the beauty of menopause and the marvels of menstruation, but this is no more necessary than hanging on to the witch who bears a curse. Somewhere between the goddess and the demon is the menstruating woman and after her the woman at menopause—living women with cycles of life not experienced by men, different and equal.'

While admirable in its attempts to break existing medical models, this approach is still too narrow and confined, limiting the menopause to a female cycle rather than to the human cycle of ageing generally and creating a new myth, of the 'Sexual Forever' woman. Thus Paula Weideger suggests that the traditional and acceptable formula of old man with young girl is actually, in purely biological terms, the wrong way round, for 'In purely sexual terms . . . the young man is likely to find in his older partner a woman who has realised her capacity for sexual response, while the young woman is likely to find in her older partner a man who has a diminished capacity for sexual response'. The woman, we are assured, has not lost *her* sexuality but the man has lost a great deal of his sexual interest in her. She concludes with the sad but necessarily true fact that biology 'is often twisted or obliterated to serve social ends'. Exactly. We cannot think of sexuality in purely biological terms, assuming it's usually a two-way process between two people—i.e., *social*. If the man then loses interest in the older woman's sexuality can we still talk of it as sexuality? Or does this once again reduce her body to a 'machine à plaisir' equally serviced by a vibrator or masturbation, as advocated by the current sex therapists? Just how much it depends on *two* people is assessed by Simone de Beauvoir when she writes on the ageing woman's sexuality (and here one feels she is speaking from bitter experience):

'If he goes on desiring her she easily puts up with her body's ageing. But at the first sign of coldness she feels her ugliness in all its horrors, she is disgusted with her image and cannot bear to expose her poor person to others.'

Whereas the older woman until recently was held to be sexually 'invisible' the new mythology represents her as voracious; the women's magazines are full of ageing actresses and their young husbands or lovers; socialites and ladies of the royal blood with their young companions. Older women, we are told, are back in demand. But they always were when they went hand in hand with wealth, status or power. Ageing charwomen don't marry young viscounts or pop-stars, just as male old-age pensioners don't land eighteen-year-old blonde models. Sex always entails *exchange* of more than a biological kind. Sexuality cannot be said to exist without this notion of exchange. Unless the whole of the female population suddenly assumes massive power and rank, as well as wealth, woman will continue to remain largely sexually invisible with old age.

This is partly related to the ambiguity of her position—as the Life-giver, she is also the Death-bringer. Many societies have legends which deal with the ability of young female bodies to impart youth and virtue to ageing males; and conversely, with the old woman, as the Bringer of Death. Experiments with rats have indeed shown that a single young female put among ageing male rats, improves their condition, and gives them greater chance for survival. Gerocomy (this idea) lives on in the comic television caricatures of today— all the 'dirty old men' who rub up against nubile young nurses, secretaries and shop assistants. Whereas the 'witch' image— the 'death' image—of the older woman dies hard, and we are given harridans in hairnets. The few women who defeat the stereotype are those of remarkable achievement or power— Marie Rambert, Golda Meir or the Queen Mother, or those who unflinchingly cling to a facsimile of youth—Mae West, Gloria Swanson or Marlene Dietrich. Simone de Beauvoir goes as far as to claim that 'no one ever speaks of a "beautiful old woman" '; but this perhaps reflects her own Gallic prejudices rather than anything else.

Why then are old women condemned to a more savage stereotype than old men, who may be called 'lechers' or 'fools' but rarely suffer the indignity of 'old bag'? 'As she gets older,' writes Germaine Greer in *The Female Eunuch*, 'the imagery becomes more repellent; she becomes obese, her breasts grow huge and sagging, the curlers are never out of her hair; her voice is louder and more insistent; finally she is transformed into that most hated female image of all, the wife's mother, the ubiquitous mother-in-law.' Both men and women in our society are condemned toward the end of their lives to becoming 'unpersons', but women bear the additional brunt of supposed malevolent powers—of the 'old witch' image. The mother-in-law is not only universally crudely caricatured, but 'mother-in-law avoidance' (ranging from actual physical avoidance by either son- or daughter-in-law to formalised 'joking relationships') is fairly universal. Women are not alone, as Simone de Beauvoir suggests, in being condemned to 'weave the very nothingness of her days' in old age; both men and women suffer the 'ejection from a citizenship traditionally based on work', and are forced to suffer 'demeaning idleness' and 'non-use'. Why then is the old woman alone cast as the witch? Does witchcraft equal womancraft as has been claimed by some writers, and is it feared for these reasons? I would tend to take a more sociological viewpoint (i.e., looking at witchcraft in terms of who accuses whom) and go along with Mary Douglas who equates witchcraft, like all 'pollution', with areas of ambiguity:

'Where the social system requires people to hold dangerously ambiguous roles, these persons are credited with uncontrolled, unconscious, dangerous, disapproved powers —such as witchcraft and evil-eye.' Witchcraft accusations are 'a means of exerting control where practical forms of control are difficult. Witchcraft, then, is found in the non-structure. Witches are social equivalents of beetles and spiders who live in the cracks of the walls and wainscoting. They attract the fears and dislikes which other ambiguities and contradictions attract in other thought structures, and the kind of powers attributed to them symbolize their ambiguous, inarticulate status.'

This would to some extent explain why older women are

still the witches of our society, described as hags by those who
would control them with hormones. They occupy the cracks
of our social structure (think of most widows and their raw
deal) but because, and this is a big because, they outlive men
and often go on to acquire their property, they have an
ambiguous power.

As Arianna Stassinopoulos points out in *The Female Woman*:

'If women remain an underclass in industrial societies,
they must be the only such group that lives longer, owns
more wealth, and enjoys more deference than its
oppressors.'

It is possible that if nature were to retract woman's evolutionary
advantage she would cease to be thought of as a source of
psychic malevolence. To narrow the source of her 'witchiness'
to menstruation or the menstrual or menopausal taboo is to
fail to recognize the connection with the wider taboo system,
and above all the taboo of death.

We no longer have the sexual taboos of the 19th century
but our industrialized society, with the concomitant decline
of religion and theory of an after-life, has bred its own taboos.
Geoffrey Gorer in *Death, Grief and Mourning in Contemporary
Britain* puts it thus:

'It seems possible to trace a connection between the shift
of taboos and the shift in religious beliefs. In the 19th
century most of the inhabitants of Protestant countries
seem to have subscribed to the Pauline beliefs in the
sinfulness of the body and the certainty of the after life . . .
It was possible to insist on the corruption of the dead
body, and the dishonour of its begetting, while there was a
living belief in the incorruption and the glory of the
immortal part. But, in England at any rate, belief in the
future life as taught in Christian doctrine is very un-

common today even in the minority who make church-
going or prayer a consistent part of their lives, and without
some such belief natural death and physical decomposition
have become too horrible to contemplate or discuss.'

Old women are horrible, just as death is horrible; we fear
them because they are visible reminders that death may come
out at any time and 'call us to bed'. Myth always mediates
realities. It softens the blow. It grants the impossible. But one
must beware of giving it a literal meaning. It is remarkable
how consistent the myths are: eternal youth, witches, sexual
libertines. These are recurrent themes in world history. Our
technical society has generated its own myths; we promise the
elderly freedom from pain and disease, and a medical attendant
at their death-bed, but on the other hand we condemn them
to social death long before physical death as social identity is
almost entirely 'work' based. As I. M. Lewis writes in *Social
Anthropology in Perspective*:

'In tribal societies it is evident that what we may call
social death follows *physical* death. In our modern welfare
conditions, however, men often retire gracefully from
active life becoming socially dead while they are physically
very much alive ... our attenuated mortuary rituals
seem to reflect this brusque disjunction and make the
brute fact of physical death even more grotesque and
obscenely embarrassing.'

Writers such as Simone de Beauvoir in *The Second Sex* tend
to assume a very superior and negative attitude towards the
'fancy' work of the older woman:

'Here we come upon the sorry tragedy of the older
woman; she realises she is useless, all her life long the
middle-class woman has often had to solve the ridiculous

problem of how to kill time. But when the children are grown, the husband a made man or at least settled down, the time must still be killed somehow. Fancy work was invented to mask their horrible idleness; hands embroider, they knit, they are in motion. This is no real work, for the object reproduced is trifling, and to know what to do with it is often a problem ... This is no longer a game that in its uselessness expressed the pure joy of living; and it is hardly an escape, since the mind remained vacant. It is the "absurd amusement" described by Pascal; with the needle or the crochet hook, woman sadly weaves the very nothingness of her days.'

But many men would be only too glad to have even this 'absurd amusement'. De Beauvoir, too, falls into the modern trap of separating 'public' from 'private', of 'real' work from 'non-real' work. It could be in the future that we will break the pernicious divisions between 'public' and 'private' and all work, at home, in the garden, on the allotment, will be *work*, and the old will be able to salvage some of their dignity in this work. When this happens you may be sure both men and women will no longer suffer from 'menopausal' symptoms. As Alex Comfort has said, 'Either we reprogramme society to find new engagement for the people it dumps or we declare them unpeople and discover a stack of bogus-science grounds for believing that ineptitude, non-humanness, dependency, unintelligence and lack of dignity start at thirty-nine.'

Unfortunately we have chosen to do the latter, largely because we stand in thrall to our technological consciousness and its concomitant social organization of the small nuclear family, with its ethic of individualism which teaches its members to be ashamed of dependency.

Women in one sense are more fortunate than men: their body cycles give them a marker, an acute awareness of their social position. The menopause has made many women realize that it is not physical symptoms alone they are dealing with, but social status and role in life generally. As long as they are not seduced by hormone mythology or any other, it may give them the impetus to do something about it. Men's 'menopausal' symptoms are less well-defined and more gradual, but there are signs that they too are becoming aware of their ejection from personhood in old age.

One possible solution suggests itself for both men and women —one which derives from the very condition which promotes loneliness and low status in old age—the breakdown of the family. Family breakdown has placed thousands of children in care (50,000 in Great Britain in 1979) just as we place our old in institutions. At both ends of the cycle, we have our unpersons. Two negatives might just make a positive. If we could encourage our elderly to foster the young in care, we would be providing a much needed role for the old as surrogate grandparents, as well as care for the neglected young.

If technology cannot provide or makes it impossible to have an eschatology, it could possibly provide some new social forms which would allow people to function more wholly during their limited lifetimes. Welfare was one such promise but it, too, took its cue from a fragmented society with a fragmented consciousness, and did little to relate parts of the society.

In the United States, artificial communities for the old have held out the same promises, but they too only succeed in creating more isolation and alienation.

The old have been socially aged in our society through lack of role: in traditional, pre-literate societies, they were the books, the walking genealogies, the repositories of knowledge, serving as links with the past as well as with the future. The motion was a circular one: as a person came closer towards death, he gained in esteem, as he came closer to the status of ancestor, he became the guardian of society, and thus he was increasingly feared and respected. Time is no longer circular for us: it has a curious one-dimensional aspect; if we live in the future, it is our children's future; the old represent the Void.

CHAPTER 7

The Depressed Body or the Invisible Woman

'Depression is withheld knowledge.'

John Layard

' *"In all sadness there would be profit"* . . . *therefore, no person should feel depressed, nor should his heart become exceedingly troubled, even though he is engaged all his days in this conflict, for perhaps because of this he was created and this is his service—constantly to subjugate the* sitra ahra (*the "other side"*).'

Rabbi Schneur Zalman of Liadi, *The Tanya*

'Increasingly, we come to know real privacy, real space in which to experiment with our sensibility, only in extreme disguises: nervous breakdown, addiction, economic failure.'

George Steiner, *Language and Silence*

One of the great unexplained mysteries of medical history is that one hundred or years ago, something called *hysteria* was frequently found among women—so frequently, that Sigmund Freud based practically all his theories upon his encounters with middle-aged, 'hysterical' Viennese ladies. Today hysteria is rare and has been replaced by another syndrome known as depression, in company with anxiety, as the most common form of mental illness that women fall prey to.[1]

Although there is no precise agreement on the definition of these two terms and both, of course, in common with all classifications of mental illness or disorder, have been used as virtual rag-bags for any unexplained conditions, we know that they are at *different ends of the spectrum*. They both have a very different 'feel' to them. Hysteria is one of the oldest concepts in medicine: at the time of Hippocrates traditional theory had it that hysteria was a disease of the uterus which wandered about the body, causing a multitude of complaints. It was thought to manifest itself in anything from diarrhoea to backache, from coughs to fits, and was most commonly

[1] E. Slater and V. Cowrie in *The Genetics of Mental Disorders* calculated from admission statistics for England and Wales that the morbid rate for affective psychoses up to the age of 75 years is 5.8   for females, 3.5   for males. The increased female risk is for unipolar depressive illnesses.

associated with leisured women. It was not until the 19th century, when Charcot's experiments showed that hysterical conditions such as paralysis or mutism could be made to disappear under hypnosis, that it gained its status as a mental illness, and it was seen as a 'dissociative' state similar in kind to the 'possession' or 'trance' states of some other societies where it was often connected with religious ceremonies.

In the popular mind, however, hysteria has always been associated with 'throwing fits', with shrieking, uncontrollable women subject to violent and abusive outbursts—something between the Devils of Loudun and the Taming of the Shrew. J. K. Wing, a distinguished professor at the Institute of Psychiatry, writes about the hysterical personality thus:

> 'Far from accepting their given dispositions and life opportunities, hysterical personalities crave to appear, both to themselves and others, as *more than they are* [my emphasis], and to experience more than they are ever capable of. The place of genuine experience and natural expression is usurped by a contrived stage-act, a forced kind of experience. This is not contrived "consciously" but reflects the ability of the true hysteric to live wholly in his own drama, be caught up entirely for the moment and to succeed in seeming genuine.'

If hysteria has to do with *drama*, and making *too* much of things, depression on the other hand, means *underplaying*, and seeing things as *less* than they are, especially the self. Thus in his remarkable account, *Breakdown*, Stuart Sutherland describes his own depression:

> 'Apart from feelings of utter despondency, worthlessness, guilt, and the loss of self-regard, it may, as in my case, be accompanied by extreme agitation and anxiety. In addition there is usually a loss of appetite for both food and sex

and there are difficulties in sleeping. In some depressives, thought processes and bodily movements are greatly slowed down: they may adopt a glazed facial expression and reply to questions only after a long interval and then in an almost inaudible voice.'

If hysterics, then, want to appear 'more than they are', depressives, with their downcast looks, round-shouldered posture, and inaudible voices, wish to appear *less* than they are.

Why should both conditions be associated with women? Statistics today show that more than twice as many women are treated for depression as men. This depression may vary in kind from what is known as housewives' blues, post-natal depression, depression associated with pre-menstrual tension, even slight anxiety, to full-blown psychotic depression, but as Sutherland writes, 'the borderline between "normal" depression and pathological depression warranting drug treatment is often hard to draw'. And the brutal fact remains that a very high proportion of women are taking anti-depressants or tranquillizing drugs of some sort—according to a survey in *Woman's Own* magazine in May 1978, as many as 25 per cent of women. In 1975, anti-depressants cost the National Health Service £12,063,000, with the vast majority going to women.

Women, then, have switched from the hysterical class, to the depressed class, and, indeed, to the drugged class. What has changed in women's condition to make them so much more susceptible to depression and, indeed, mental illness generally? Various theories have been advanced which fall into one of three categories. First, psycho-analytic theories which see depression in terms of *repression* and which are outside the scope of this chapter. Second, the ever-popular *stress* theory: 'stress' consisting of anything from overwork, unhappy marriage death in the family, to overcrowded living and poor housing.

The third is the almost equally popular 'scapegoat' theory. Women are *de*pressed because they are *op*pressed. This is the approach not only of 'radical' psychiatry but of various writers ranging from Fritz Perls ('depression is hidden resentment') to R. D. Laing, and has been echoed by feminists who denounce the social conditions that drive women into depression and anxiety, and see only a total change *in society* as the remedy. Some see the oppression coming from the *family* itself, some from the individual's resentment, and others from *society*.

All these approaches are valid to some extent: depression may be due to repressions, stress, loss, hidden anger, resentment, oppression, alienation as well as a number of other factors, genetic, biochemical, or environmental, which I have not mentioned. However, as Sutherland so aptly points out, apart from these concepts not being in the slightest bit useful to those in the throes of depression (who needs to be told that *society* needs changing when in their darkest depths?), there seems to be a contorted logic, or rather lack of logic about the whole question of women and depression.

If women really do suffer from depression because of oppression, we ought to be examining societies where there is even more oppression (difficult though it is to define), where there is no relief from hard, physical labour, dangerous childbirth, disease; where women are shackled with pollution taboos, tied to a 'feminine role' of utter drudgery and relentless childbearing, and have no opportunity to participate in public life; and see if their incidence of depression is higher than our own. We ought then to look at societies where women are more 'liberated' than our own—socialist countries, where equal opportunity in education and jobs exists—and see if their incidence of depression is any *lower*. We ought then to see if there is *any* society, or section of society where women do not suffer from depression, and try to isolate the special contributing factors.

For in a study of mental illness it is just as important to look at those who are healthy and ask what brings that about. Unfortunately this is all too rarely done: we are so used to looking for signs of sickness that the idea of making a study of health, of the absence of sickness, is completely alien to us. If we bandy words like 'stress', 'deprivation' and 'oppression', we must ask, or at least wonder, why, if all of us are exposed to equal, or near-equal amounts of stress (and deprivation too, is only a relative concept), why do only some of us succumb? To answer that some people are more vulnerable, or more disposed to react in certain ways, only leads us back to square one.

A cursory glance around varying societies plainly shows that oppression does not necessarily equal depression, which on the contrary seems to have a higher frequency in those societies where women have achieved a greater level of emancipation (e.g., the United States, Great Britain and Sweden). Depressive illness has traditionally been reported as infrequent in developing countries[1] and some writers have pointed to socio-cultural factors to account for this; others to diagnostic differences. I would go one step further and try to relate this low incidence to clearly defined role and personal space. To be fair, all that this may perhaps demonstrate is the difficulty of defining notions of oppression and emancipation. We meet the same dilemma when coming across the rare society that has no depression at all (or virtually none), such as certain religious communities, but which have, from an objective viewpoint, a high degree of oppression.

Faced with these problems, I have decided to view the subject from another perspective entirely: that of visibility and invisibility, or to put it another way, that of personal space. For I feel that the whole problem of depression is linked to that of space.

First, a definition of personal space. Personal space refers to an area with invisible boundaries surrounding a person's body into which intruders may not come. It has also been described

---

[1] See G. A. German, *Aspects of Clinical Psychiatry in Sub-Saharan Africa* and B. Prince, *The Changing Picture of Depressive Syndromes in Africa*.

as *portable territory*, since the individual carries it with him wherever he goes, although it disappears under certain conditions such as crowding. Experiments have shown that when an individual's personal space is invaded (and several things can constitute 'territorial encroachment', from physical violation to noise), the most extreme reaction is, as with animals, one of *flight*. Sociologists Lyman and Scott have identified one form of territorial encroachment which they call 'contamination', whereby a territory is rendered impure with respect to its definition and usage, and this is the situation described graphically by Mary Douglas in the introduction to her book *Purity and Danger*:

> 'I am personally rather tolerant of disorder. But I always remember how unrelaxed I felt in a particular bathroom which was kept spotlessly clean in so far as the removal of grime and grease was concerned. It had been installed in an old house in a space created by the simple expedient of setting a door at each end of a corridor between two staircases. The decor remained unchanged: the engraved portrait of Vinogradoff, the books, the gardening tools, the row of gumboots. It all made good sense as the scene of a back corridor, but as a bathroom—the impression destroyed repose.'

Many modern kitchens, bedrooms and bathrooms 'destroy repose' and above all make for contamination of territory, or invasion of personal space.

That men suffer less in this respect than women is perhaps because they do not feel their personal space to be invaded in the same way insofar as the woman is often regarded as a non-person, and in Robert Sommer's words, 'A non-person cannot invade someone's personal space any more than a tree or chair can'. Studies in mental hospitals have shown that mental patients always try to seek out some individual territory, often, for the lack of any other facilities, locking themselves in linen cupboards or unused rooms, sitting on the backs of fire-escapes, etc. This is indicative of the fundamental human need for personal space, free from invasion. (Dr Wellington Hung at the Maudsley Hospital, London, attributes the rise in the incidence of agoraphobia among women to a similar cause: he said recently that he felt sure there was a connection between modern woman's 'fear of open spaces' and the lack of space she experienced in her daily life.)

On another level, the growing popularity of yoga and trans-cendental meditation could possibly be interpreted as an attempt to create 'inner' personal space, in the event of invasion from without.

But to go back to the two polar concepts of hysteria and depression. If hysteria means too much self, and depression, too little, we can go on from there, and posit that whereas Victorian women, by virtue of their limited role in society, *felt themselves to be invisible and used hysteria to make themselves visible, contemporary woman feels herself to be too visible, and attempts to make herself invisible.*

It has long been recognized that many kinds of mental illness can be bids for power. Anthropologists have been even readier to acknowledge this than psychiatrists. Hysteria in other societies is often manifest in such things as spirit possession, trance or 'speaking in tongues'. The anthropologist Ioan Lewis describes the situation among the Muslim Somali of north-east Africa where 'married women are frequently prone to mysterious complaints which are diagnosed by the experts as possession by evil spirits. These latter are exceedingly de-manding; treatment consists of discovering their requirements and agreeing to them on condition that the human victim is released from their power. It is a striking fact, by no means lost on the men who have to pay for them, that the spirits which so plague their women-folk have expensive tastes and invariably request such items as costly perfumes, jewellery, fine dresses, and delicious foods and sweetmeats.' He then goes on to ask why women should resort to such devious tactics. The reason is partly because 'in this particular society men rule the roost and women have low status and few rights they can directly exercise. Divorce is common and easily obtained by men; women can only achieve it with difficulty. So with the legal dice against them, women are forced to adopt such oblique means of redress and appeal as possession "illnesses". Through the effects which it exerts on men, spirit-possession is in fact one of the most prized and successful weapons at the disposal of Somali women.'

It is not difficult to discern a similar pattern here to the one which existed in Victorian England, when, indeed, there was a proliferation of female spirit mediums, as well as a wide range of women's 'weapon' illnesses which included fainting fits, what is termed 'neurasthenia'—i.e., general listlessness, head-aches and irritability—as well as hysteria.

If hysteria, then, in common with spirit possession, rep-resented a bid for power in an oppressive society, what does depression represent—or why, for that matter, did women's illness change its nature so entirely? Unless one contends that it is merely a question of labelling, which I do not, as the symptoms are so obviously different, though labelling does have something to do with it. Are women speaking a different language, but saying the same thing? Or are they saying something else in a society which has given them their freedom, removed the corsets and crinolines, but with it, *taken away their woman's space*?

One of the literal meanings of depressed is 'made concave'. Now, to be made concave means to be hollowed out, i.e., a space is made, an indentation where previously there was none. I believe that all depression is an attempt to make a space for oneself—finding a place to retreat to—albeit within oneself—a place to be and re-summon enough energy to enter the world again. This applies as much to post-natal depression as it does to premenstrual or menopausal depression; to depression caused by loss or change in status. At all these times woman needs a refuge, sanctuary, as it were, and through depression could find it within herself if she were allowed to come to terms with it. It is more than merely 'time-out'; it represents a bid for privacy, for freedom from exposure.

The assault upon privacy could well be one of the defining features of contemporary society for both men and women. Women, to a large extent, have suffered more than men in this respect: not only has her body been demystified, analysed, fragmented, and reassembled on the factory line, her physical spaces have been taken away from her: the Victorian woman at least had the kitchen, music-room and sewing-room as her own domain. Today, with open-plan design, it is rare that a woman has any place to be even in her own home; her husband may have a workshop, a developing room, a den, a study or a studio, but she is lucky usually if she gets the box-room shared with a load of junk. Even the kitchen is designed so that she can cook in full view of the guests, and it is more than likely invaded at all times by teenage children, toddlers and husband. Kitchens used to be private places, marvellous 'hearts of the home', that only the woman and her servants (if she had any) could penetrate. They were placed at the back of the house (or in the basement) so that they were as removed as possible, as private as possible, from the front room, the public face of the house. Today, it is trendy to be led straight into the kitchen which is smartly done up with fancy tiles and jars, less for functional than for decorative purposes. In fact many women, in spite of the radical chic element in it, are made distinctly nervous by having to assemble cordon bleu dishes (and promptly clear away) in party gear *in front of* their guests.

Where can women 'be', then? What does our society offer in the way of a retreat? Paradoxically, as the status of women supposedly is seen to rise, their personal space is rapidly shrinking. It is true that everyone's personal space has been diminished in the modern world as a result or over-population and overcrowding. On the other hand there are areas where women's space has virtually been wiped off the map. I am thinking of the large, comfortable 'powder rooms' and ladies' waiting-rooms still found in old-fashioned station hotels. It is well known from studies in spatial behaviour that if a person (or animal) wanders into someone else's personal space, he or she tries to make himself or herself invisible. My impression is that today women are continually wandering into men's space and making themselves invisible through depression.

There are, of course, some places that *are* considered women's retreats: shops, beauty-salons, and mother and child groups. The first two, although certainly related to '*time-out*', because of their commercial pressuring offer very little in the way of retreat and true refreshment. Although it is true that mother and child groups provide needed contact and friendships, they can scarcely be called relaxing or resuscitating. True, too, there is a growing number of 'Women's Groups' inspired by the idea of 'Sisterhood' (which at the same time as recognizing the problem, compounds it by denying women some of their traditional 'spaces'). These groups may even sustain and provide inspiration, warmth and comradeship for a while, but they do not meet the requirements of true sanctuary, for true sanctuary requires not only a physical place to be, but accompanying *ritual* devices (for instance, baths in Moslem society) to help the woman 'profit from her sadness'. Space is in the mind as well as on the ground.

Drugs may help alleviate the symptoms of depression but they in no way provide a true cure as they tend to close one in on oneself more, while at the same time depleting one's physical energy. Hospitals, with their largely bleak, un-attractive surroundings and poor food, cannot meet the requirements of retreat either, although they are often used as 'pseudo'-sanctuaries by women. How often have I heard the pregnant mother say, 'I look forward to going into hospital for a nice rest?' which, in view of the fact that hospitals rouse you at dawn and are a hub of ceaseless and often irritating activity, is somewhat to be wondered at. Do women innately recognize the need they have for periodic sanctuary to aid both physical and spiritual readjustment?

Depression, as a *bid for space* and sanctuary, has as yet gone unrecognized by psychiatrists, even when they consider its *social* dimensions. While recent studies, such as '*Social Origins of Depression, a Study of Psychiatric Disorder in Women*' by G. W. Brown and T. Harris, recognize some of the environmental factors—for instance, bad housing, financial difficulties, and general lack of intimate relationship—that may influence a woman's response to traumatic events and result in depression, they still beg the questions: why 'problems of living' affect some women more than others; why some women in some societies, living in materially appalling conditions, have managed to survive with a relatively low incidence of depression.

Some years ago, while living with a group of people known as the Lubavitch Hassidim in the borough of Hackney, a relatively deprived and decaying inner London area, I was struck how infrequently I ever encountered depression. In spite of very large families (by modern standards), relatively bad housing, frequently low incomes, poor diet (and there is a school of thought which sees diet as all), and often histories that somewhere included labour or concentration camps, there was an unusual cheerfulness, and even—I use an old-fashioned word—'gaiety' about the women, most of whom had never heard of post-natal depression, let alone experienced it. 'We are not allowed to be depressed,' they would tell me, 'it is the worst thing. If you start to feel depressed you must read the "Tanya"[1]—there are special portions.' Nor did they wear the fixed smiles of women 'grinning and bearing it'; they laughed often and easily, and for women who by modern standards

[1] The *Tanya* is another name for the philosophical work by Rabbi Schneur Zalman, the founder of the Hassidic group. Its other name is *Liqqutei Amarim*.

were severely restricted in everything they did, from how they dressed, in puritanically modest clothing, to the rigid dietary restrictions placed upon them, and who were never once able to stray from their 'woman's space' in this sexually segregated society, they showed a remarkable energy, spontaneity and ease of manner. Many with five or more children attended study groups, held down jobs, kept all the minutiae of ritual within the home, including cooking for armies on frequent Holy Days, and took part in the 'conversionist', missionizing activity which is the particular domain of this group. I remember one woman who literally forty-eight hours after the birth of a fifth child, came rushing, dishevelled, into a study group, having stayed up the night before between breast feeding to study the text. Wig[1] askew, leaking milk, she looked radiant.

When I returned home at weekends I would compare them with the listless middle-class wives I knew, struggling with one or maybe two children, plagued by headaches, depression and 'the wrong time of the month', and forever engaged in fruitless searches for the right au-pair, extra-mural course, husband or job, anything which would once and for all release them from the tedium of their lives. Many, it is true, had part-time, or even full-time jobs, entertained regularly, and even took further academic degrees, but few managed to feel free of resentment toward both husband and children, and exuded about as much joy and energy as an Aspirin advertisement.

The working-class women I knew, *even though* they had the support of mum round the corner, took 'tablets' for everything from backache to 'nerves', and essentially came no nearer to presenting a picture of sweetness and light. In fact, according to statistics they are four times more likely than their middle-class sisters to suffer depression. Later on, as an ante-natal teacher who taught literally hundreds of women of all classes,

---

[1] Women of this group shave their heads on marrying and henceforth wear wigs, ('sheytels').

I realized that *all* of them, without exception, suffered or claimed to suffer from depression. To be a woman was to be depressed. I have overheard girls as young as 6 or 7 saying, 'I'm depressed today, mummy.' What have we done to produce such dour womanhood?

My lovely happy ladies of Hackney must have had something we didn't have. And they did: apart from religion, they had *space* as women—clearly demarcated areas where they reigned supreme; they knew they were as essential in the cosmological scheme of things as men—even as they peeled the potatoes they were making something happen in heaven; they had enormous support from one another; as they were all working toward a common goal, neighbours would not hesitate to babysit, or take in and feed another child; they had that enviable thing called '*Gemeinschaft*'—a community of like-minded people; they had rituals which gave them outlets for emotion; song and dance (albeit in separate male/female groups), and, if incipient depression did creep in, special techniques to deal with it—chants and tracts.

Similarly, no doubt, one could turn to communities of nuns, Jehovah's Witnesses or other religious sects, where cheerfulness is considered a virtue, and depression non-existent. And, my critics will add, if you 'get religion' of course depression will go. While certainly not denying the importance of the specifically religious or ideological element (and into this category, no doubt, would come the USSR and China and other socialist communities, and I am not suggesting that we all get to a nunnery), I feel that mental health within these groups is as much facilitated by the *social structure* (e.g., the rigid separation of men and women and their roles), and the accompanying ritual, as by the ideological imperatives ('Thou shalt not be depressed'). A society which places a great value on social cohesion would find depression particularly threatening, as it tends to place the individual for a while outside society and to break down categories in much the same way as suicide (its often logical conclusion) and, in some respects, in much the same way as hysteria or spirit possession—except that in the latter case there is often a distinct bid for power, whereas in the case of depression it is less *power* than invisibility.

In our society we have removed the *moral* element from depression (it is rarely considered a sin), and replaced it with a medical model. In doing so, however, we have not made provisions, in the same way that traditional religions have, for its opposite (and indeed its prevention), i.e., cheerfulness, and mental health; for medicine generally is not predisposed to studying *health*. While I believe it is partly caused, for women, by lack of space, and the consequent retreat into oneself, I believe, too, that we should be looking at other elements, especially the role of suggestion. I believe that in our society generally women are being deflected from the true problem of what constitutes their depression, i.e., lack of space, and *are being conditioned to accept depression as their lot*, just as a century or so ago, they were conditioned to accept hysteria, and just as in religious societies women are conditioned to be cheerful. Certainly their tolerance for suffering and pain seems to have been drastically reduced.

Today, women are educated for childbirth, and one thing they are all automatically taught is to expect drastic fluctuations in hormones and mood both during pregnancy and after— but especially after, and, generally, a whole class in ante-natal courses is devoted to post-natal depression. There are plays, books and a wealth of literature on the subject. (It has occurred to me, too, that the increasing incidence of post-natal depression might relate to the father's increasing role in childbirth and child rearing, where woman's space has been further encroached on.) Although hormonal determinism is commonly taught, women are rarely told that they can to some extent *control* their own hormones, that it is not simply a one-way process.

I am convinced that it is possible through careful diet, and especially the use of certain vitamin supplements such as Vitamin E, plus certain relaxation techniques, to regulate one's own hormone level. One expectant mother (herself an ante-natal teacher) came to me for advice because her hormone level was fluctuating wildly during pregnancy. Her own doctor had prescribed artificial hormones which only served to add other unpleasant side effects and raise her blood pressure. He had failed to notice her general run-down appear-ance and obesity, which were indications of some breakdown in the total bodily system, as was her general state of mind, which was full of death fantasies and exaggerated paranoic fears.

I managed to convert her to a wholefood diet, consisting of a high proportion of fruit and vegetables, pure fruit juices, an extra 20 grams of protein (in the form of oily fish rather than meat), and a supplement of 400 i.u. Vitamin E per day. She also learned special body awareness exercises and relaxation techniques, and some light toning exercises. She became proud and aware of her body for the first time during pregnancy. Necessary, too, were exercises for the expression of anger to release hostile feelings she had towards an alcoholic father, which were all emerging during pregnancy. Her hormone level gradually became normal and stable. Her hair and skin took on a new lustre and fine texture. She lost weight and, most dramatically of all, was able to give birth to her son naturally (her obstetrician had foreseen a Caesarian section). Thus a combination of therapy, diet and exercise had restored her body to a healthy functioning.

Latest scientific research points to the way the brain, via the glands, can control hormonal activity. Expectation may have much to do with it: I have often had mothers coming to me and saying, with some surprise, 'But I wasn't depressed. Wasn't I supposed to be?'

Schoolgirls are taught to expect a ghastly monthly 'low' which will render them susceptible to anything from kleptomania to nymphomania, which experts label the pre-menstrual syndrome. In a recent television chat show devoted to the subject, one woman, when asked about her pre-menstrual tension and how long it lasted, replied in all earnestness, 'Three weeks in every month.' Women are progressively taught to recognize teenage blues, baby blues, housewife blues, and menopausal blues. At each crucial stage of their lives they are taught to expect and recognize depression, just as, at every stage of their lives, people generally are taught to recognize illness and abnormality rather than health. Illich talks of this in *Limits to Medicine* as 'social iatrogenesis':

> 'A term designating all impairments to health that are due precisely to those socio-economic transformations which have been made attractive, possible, or necessary by the institutional shape health care has taken ... It obtains when medical bureaucracy creates ill-health by increasing stress, by multiplying disabling dependence, by generating new painful needs, by lowering the levels of tolerance for discomfort or pain, by reducing the leeway that people are wont to concede to an individual when he suffers, and by abolishing even the right to self-care.'

We can learn from societies which insist that depression is the responsibility first and foremost of the individual, while recognizing its potential for social ill or good; which provide the individual with techniques to deal with it; which recognize its positive potential; and above all, which give their individuals space in which to come to terms with it.

Perhaps the reason why so many more women than men present themselves in doctors' surgeries with 'depressive' symptoms and are quick to reach for the pills, is that (a) they have been taught to a greater degree than men to interpret all their symptoms as depression; (b) they have virtually no ritual outlets e.g., sports, clubs, pubs and places to be, generally; (c) they have fewer emotional outlets for the expression of anger. It is still harder for women to express anger than for men. I have been struck by this simple fact time and time again when dealing with depression in pregnant women. When I tell the tight-lipped women in my classes that they must give vent to their anger, slam a few doors, smash a few glasses, pummel pillows or whatever, the results are often dramatic. 'I've been foul all week to everyone, but at least my depression has lifted,' is something I hear frequently.

Not all that we call depression is hidden anger, but the expression of anger, as opposed to petulance, can often prove very cathartic.

Men may be as potentially prone to depression as women, but society is on their side in providing many more ways for them to deal with it, both preventive and expressive, ranging from the rituals of sport to greater allowance of personal space.

If I have given the impression that I have failed to acknowledge the very real anguish and pain of depression, this is unintentional: I know from my own experience and those of the women I teach that the suffering is very real. I have merely been questioning the interpretation given to depression, and the wisdom of much current education which teaches women to *expect* it without suggesting any preventive measures or providing any real cures, and refusing to recognize its 'negative energy' side. There are two slight glimmers of hope on the horizon: the first is the fact that some psycho-therapy (notably the Behaviourist school, which claims that all is performance, and that performance itself it merely a complicated pattern of inevitable responses to preceding stimuli), is returning to the old-fashioned ideas of self-control and will-power, making extensive use of suggestion. Transcendental Meditation, Biofeedback and Yoga use similar techniques encouraging people in control over their own bodies, and to make a space for themselves mentally.

One theory put forward by Martin P. Seligman[1] is that depression is *learned* helplessness, and he suggests that it might be cured by increasing the patient's sense of efficacy—by teaching him that he can *control* the re-inforcers—that is that the patient should discover and come to believe that his or her responses to whatever situation produce the gratification he desires: that he or she is, in short, an effective human being.

The second glimmer of hope is dancing schools: they are enjoying a renewed popularity. I have long since held, in common with the Hassidim, that dancing is the best cure for all depression. Dance therapy is now commonplace in mental hospitals everywhere. But dance as a preventive measure—a mental hygiene—has been less commented upon. The mid to late thirties seems to be a time for women when they are seized by the urge to dance, and an increasing number join their local tap dance or modern ballet class. Dance, unlike sport, is generally non-competitive, and purely expressive. Like sport it has its ritual elements, is physically demanding, and requires perfect body control and coordination. Sport may well have its symbolic aspects, but dance constitutes a complete language, and many women are turning to this language as the semantic matrix proves more and more limiting. Dancing reinstates the individual again in the world and links him to its innumerable rhythms. 'Dancing for joy is the highest manifestation of the most intense feeling of inner happiness, a feeling which permeates the entire body, from head to foot,' according to the Hassidim. When all women dance, there will be less depression.

Some religions traditionally provided 'retreats' for the spiritually anguished where they were able to reniew themselves. Part of the renewal was based on lovingly prepared food, the beauty of natural surroundings, isolation from the pressures of the world, and the non-invasion of privacy and personal space that the rule of silence which often prevailed

[1] See bibliography.

implied. It is not only the battered and abused who need retreats, but all those who have found their personal spaces reduced. Society owes it to women to provide them with places where they can remain 'invisible' for a while. They might then be able to function without depression in the world and the negative energy of this weight of depression be applied to better things.

CHAPTER 8

The Abused Body

'The great majority of abusive parents are not monsters but anxious, unhappy people who care deeply about their success as parents and feel great guilt about the damage they do in moments of uncontrollable rage.'

R. S. Kempe and C. H. Kempe, *Child Abuse*

'From prehistoric times to the present, I believe, rape has played a critical function. It is nothing more or less than a conscious process of intimidation by which all men keep all women in a state of fear.'

Susan Brownmiller, *Against Our Will*

There are many forms that physical abuse to the body can take, but rape and battering are perhaps two which more than any others, exemplify a total breakdown of mutuality, as well as violation of the body's boundary, the maintenance of which is one of our major preoccupations. To attack our body boundary is to prevail upon our social and psychic worlds as well as our physical one. This chapter looks at some of the often conflicting beliefs underlying our conception of physical abuse, for if we look at physical abuse of the body in the varying forms of child battering and rape, it is obvious that there is a remarkable discrepancy between the two forms of abuse, even when the child abuse, as is now becoming increasingly common, takes the form of sexual violation. (R. S. Kempe and C. H. Kempe in *Child Abuse* report that between 1967 and 1972, the number of sexually abused children increased tenfold in some hospitals, and that reports of incest had reached 150 per million population in the US with massive under-reporting.) There is a discrepancy not only in our conception of the two forms of abuse—i.e., one, battering, is regarded as a disease, and the other, rape, is regarded as a crime; battering is thought to be caused by deprivation of one sort or another, while rape —unless one takes a Freudian stance which holds rape to be a perversion—belongs to the 'normal' world of male aggression less than to that of psycho-pathology. Barbara Toner in *The Facts of Rape* quotes one British psychiatrist who stresses the 'normality' of most rape offenders, and the times when 'It's perfectly normal for armies to rape whole populations of women. It's perfectly normal for men coming off a ship to get a bit tight, go around looking for girls, and, if the girls get a bit stroppy and don't come up with the goodies, it's normal for the men to take it.' The notion of deprivation does occasionally creep into the analysis of rape, as for example, when Menachem Amir in *Patterns in Forcible Rape* placed it firmly in a 'subculture of violence' and seen to be more common in deprived inner city areas, but this side of it has received less attention than the political aspects of rape: the idea that it is a conspiracy against all women by all men. There has as yet been no movement to suggest that battering is a conspiracy by all parents against all children. Most importantly, whereas in battering the parent is often absolved from all blame (and certainly the child is held to be blameless), in rape, both assailant and victim have until recently been apportioned blame, with possibly the victim coming out a little worse than her assailant. As Barbara Toner says, the belief still prevails that the victims 'go easily to the slaughter'.

Rape and battering have, of course, quite different histories; whereas as Susan Brownmiller shows in *Against Our Will* the history, legal and otherwise, of rape goes back a long way and was intricately related to marriage and property rights, 'battering' has a very recent history. It needed the invention of the X-ray to detect broken bones which had previously been diagnosed as something else like rickets or scurvy, to give it a reality. And it was only as recently as 1961, when Dr Kempe, directing a symposium conducted by the American Academy of Pediatrics, used the phrase 'battered child syndrome', that the subject took on an existence of its own. Child cruelty in many forms had been known to other centuries: as Jean Renvoize points out in *Children in Danger*, 'Victorian fathers of all social classes frequently chastized their children so severely and expected such perfection of manners from them that much of their treatment would today be classified as battering. Yet in their epoch they were seen as admirable men.' It took our century with its heightened awareness of children as individuals with rights rather than as property, to make this kind of abuse 'visible'.

Nonetheless as with rape, and to some extent mental illness, such is the difficulty with definition which is so tied to cultural norms and expectations, that its reality is still often denied. Barbara Toner, for example, writes: 'The popular view is that if the rapist cannot be labelled "fiend" or "monster" or "maniac" then he probably isn't a rapist at all.' She quotes policemen, who put it down to 'unpaid prostitution', and a Professor in Forensic Psychiatry who remarked that it must be excessively common for girls to be held down so that a man could have forcible intercourse and that rape 'as a crime' depended on 'whether the girl goes home and tells her parents who blow up, or whether she never tells anyone and puts it down to an unfortunate experience.' Just as there are those who will claim 'there is no such thing as rape', there are social workers and doctors who find difficulty in accepting the reality of battering; there are those, too, who, as in the case of rape, would see it as a crime of violence 'just like any other crime'. Jean Renvoize in *Children in Danger* quotes Detective Superintendent Roy of Northampton: 'You mustn't divorce this from other sorts of crime—when you talk about battered babies, by definition you're talking about children against whom criminal offences have been committed.'

Just as in rape, there are the problems of statistics. Any study or research done is limited by the sample: who are 'caught', who arrested, who present themselves to social workers, casualty departments, etc., and even who are overheard by the neighbours. There is the somewhat embarrassing situation that most statistics that do exist seem to indicate a link with the lower socio-economic classes, and hencc to 'the subculture of violence'. The 'subculture of violence' theory was first formulated by Marvin Wolfgang who saw social class as a prime determinant of all violent crime. Within the dominant value system of our culture there exists a subculture consisting of the poor, the disenfranchised, the deprived, the black, whose values run counter to the dominant culture, and who, when thwarted, resort to violence through lack of any other means of reaching their goals. Thus violence and aggression become a common feature of the 'subculture'. But critics are quick to point out, in both cases, that this is only because within the middle and upper classes both battering and rape are likely to go un-detected, or alternatively they will widen the concept to, for example, 'emotional battering'.

Both rape and battering include a wide range of phenomena under their aegis; in both there exists a continuum ranging from, in the case of battering, light injury to savage mutilation or even death, and in the case of rape, from 'date-rape' to rape by psychotics or gangs. Just as we are told by feminists that 'all men are rapists', we are told that 'all parents are potential batterers', but whereas we are told that all men are rapists because they hate women, we are not told that all parents are potential batterers because they hate children; on the contrary, we are told batterers really love and care about children, but suffered from 'inadequate mothering' themselves:

> 'We have seen that the great majority of abusive parents are not monsters but anxious, unhappy people who care deeply about their success as parents and feel great guilt about the damage they do in moments of uncontrollable rage. We also know that if we can manage to reach an abusive parent's memories of his own early life, often deeply buried in self-defence against intolerable depression, we are likely to find there another abused child.' (*Child Abuse*, R. S. Kempe and C. H. Kempe).

.

If both battering and rape have a chimerical quality, our attitudes toward battering are nonetheless more consistent than those toward rape. Both are based on very basic assumptions about the nature of aggression in man: Anthony Storr, in *Human Aggression*, got to the heart of the matter when he wrote of the 'aggressive response': 'What has not been decided is whether there is any pressing internal need for the mechanism to be brought into use; or whether, if the organism were never threatened, aggressive behaviour would ever be manifested,' and, most importantly, 'If the first supposition is true, what is needed to control aggression is *the provision of suitable outlets for aggression*. If the latter is true, what is required is the *avoidance of all stimuli which might arouse the aggressive response*.' Storr himself supports the view, from the wealth of evidence from animal and anthropological studies, that the organism does indeed have a 'pressing internal need' to release aggression, but this is an unpopular view, and far from providing outlets for the release of aggression, we tend to work with the second proposition—remove all stimuli, and all will be well; the idea that, given the right social conditions and early socialization, aggression would not develop in people, 'men would live in peace with one another and the millenium would at last be realized.'

Although according to Joan Cant, original head of the NSPCC Battered Child Research Department, battering is a 'potentially lethal disease' which lurks in all of us, it is only deprivation of some sort or another (sleep, mothering, housing, poverty or isolation) which will activate it. Deprivation itself is a slippery concept, always relative. As Mary Douglas writes in *Natural Symbols*:

'The argument which seeks to explain behaviour by reference to maladjustment, compensation, deprival is always fair game ... [but] he [the sociologist] *must admit it valueless for explaining negative instances* ... [my emphasis]. The deprivation hypothesis has its roots deep in our cultural heritage. Perhaps Rousseau gave the first and most emphatic vision of the individual enchained by society and liable to revolt after a certain pitch of humiliation and despair has been reached. The assumption that has bedevilled sociology ever since is that deprival and strain can be measured cross culturally.'

By the standards of Jean Liedloff's South American Indians[1] who retain close bodily contact with their mothers and the all-important 'in-arms' experiences, we are all inadequately mothered, except the fortunate few who are carried around in slings all day. Some people, however—and there are some very notable examples, like Winston Churchill—manage to turn inadequate mothering to their advantage, and end up channelling their frustrations and aggressions into worthier and more noble causes than baby-battering.

By drawing attention to our potential for battering, making it a non-taboo subject, and allowing batterers to come forward and speak, we may indeed have almost made it possible to set up a 'drag-net spreading right across the country with a mesh so fine that no parent under stress can slip through it', in Jean Renvoize's words.

On the other hand, as with all iatrogenesis, by removing the moral element we have raised levels of tolerance, and reduced sanctions for the batterer, removing much personal responsibility. We have 'normalized' battering to such an extent that it may now, contrary to the wished-for effect, be used as a *common strategy, to attract attention, as a cry for help when another cry in another language, would have been far less dangerous*. We may, in fact, have given some people this language of violence. This is not to deny that battering took place in all times and places, but simply to say that it may now be used, as there is little risk of the offender being labelled a monster or socially ostracised,

[1] See Jean Liedloff's *The Continuum Concept*, 1975.

as a form of exhibitionism—as a plea for sympathy and attention through the use of the third person, the unfortunate child.

This is suggested by many of the case histories we can now read, as so many parents seem willing, even eager, to come forward as baby-batterers. One is aware of increasing levels of sophistication, of cunning, and of knowledge of the 'listener's' expectations in these accounts. Take, for example, this extract from a case-history in Jean Renvoize's *Children in Danger*. After describing how she burnt her young son as a baby with an iron, this mother then went on to describe how, later on, when she became 'too clever' to burn him, she started to punish him in other ways:

> 'I punish him more mentally now. . . . It's cruel, I know it is. What sort of thing? Well sometimes I tell him I don't love him, or I try and frighten him. If he comes to get on my lap I push him off. It's such a pity, he's a lovely boy really and he's so affectionate. If *only* they'd do something. All they do is talk; they'll never act until I maim Paul. But I don't hit him any more so he's marked, I'm too clever for that now.'

It is almost as if the mother had read a Freudian text-book beforehand, and had calculated her effects on the interviewer, as well as on the social services: if I batter him, maim him, then I'll get my way . . .

The suspicion that battering may be being increasingly used as a strategy or a language is borne out by a lot of the evidence which shows firstly that early battering is often done in highly visible places (lips, eyes, etc.) and that most battering, contrary to expectations, takes place in families (there is little battering of illegitimate children). Could it be that unwittingly society has provided some people with a new form of communication? A shocking thought, but one that bears thinking about, especially when a review of case histories makes one aware of the depressing lack of communication between husband and wife.

Perhaps the answer lies not in trying to remove all potential stimuli of aggression, but rather in trying to provide alternative adequate means of releasing it, or providing *other channels of communication*, for battering is a form of non-verbal communication we can do without. We will not do this until we come round to agreeing that possibly part one of Storr's propositions about violence is true; until, in fact, we adjust our notion of the nature of man.

Storr's propositions could apply equally well to rape. Here the thinking is even more confused, and the apportionment of 'blame' rarely a clear-cut one. It is, in fact, riddled with double standards, double-think and general confusion often verging on hysteria. One of the reasons why there is so much confusion on the issue is because both of Storr's alternative propositions about the nature of aggression are in operation concomitantly, that is, men are thought to be inherently given to rape (i.e., 'all men are rapists') while at the same time it is felt that given the right social conditions—a non-patriarchal, non-sexist society (whatever that is)—there would be no rape, and examples are quoted almost ad nauseam of Margaret Mead's Arapesh of New Guinea, of whom she writes:

> 'Of rape the Arapesh know nothing beyond the fact that it is the unpleasant custom of the Nugum people to the southeast of them. Nor do the Arapesh have any conception of male nature that might make rape understandable to them.'

A careful re-reading of the Arapesh material shows up many features of that society that feminist writers, while admiring its Utopian qualities, have not been quick to point out: i.e., it is taboo-ridden, from the menstrual huts where each month women are isolated from puberty, to the rigid taboos, for both

men and women, surrounding the birth of a child. It is the
duty of every man and woman to scrupulously observe these
rules so that they can 'grow' children and 'grow' yams.
Margaret Mead explains it thus:

> 'There are two incompatible goods in the world: those
> associated with sex and the reproductive functions of
> women; and those associated with food, growth, and the
> hunting and gardening activities of men, which owe their
> efficacy to supernatural aids, and to the purity and growth-
> giving aspects of male blood. These two goods must be
> kept from coming into too close contact. The duty of
> every child is to grow, the duty of every man and woman
> is to observe the rules so that the children and the food
> upon which the children depend will grow.'

To the Arapesh the concepts of growth and sexual life are
antithetical. In fact the Arapesh 'do not seriously conceive of
sex outside of the marriage bond . . . Their ideal is essentially
a domestic one, not a romantic one. *Sex is a serious matter, a
matter that must be surrounded with precautions: a matter above all in
which the two partners must be of one mind*' [my emphasis].

Compare this with the situation in our society: it is hardly
similar. Secondly, writers have tended to over-emphasis the
lack of discrimination and differentiation in the upbringing of
both Arapesh boys and girls; in fact they tend to make it
appear that there are no differences at all. This, however, is
far from the case. Mead makes it clear from the outset that
'men and women do different things [albeit] for the same
reasons', and at times herself feels obliged to rationalize the
exclusion of women from different activities. Thus

> 'It is a culture in which if women are excluded from
> ceremonies it is for the sake of the women themselves not
> as a device to bolster up the pride of men, who work

desperately hard to keep the dangerous secrets that would make their wives ill and deform their unborn children.'
How, too, would the feminists like the division of labour? 'Cooking everyday food, bringing firewood and water, weeding and carrying—these are women's work; cooking ceremonial food, carrying pigs and heavy logs, house-building, sewing thatch, cleaning and fencing, carving, hunting and growing yams—these are men's work.'

Mead further tells us that with girls, 'expression of anger' is checked earlier 'to save their pretty grass skirts', whereas boys 'may roll and scream in the mud up to the age of fourteen or fifteen without any sense of shame'. Whereas girls early on learn to work cooperatively in groups, boys have exactly the opposite experience. They go off with just a father or elder brother on hunting expeditions etc. The girls learn early on to be passive and 'group'-minded, while the boys seem to have a wider range for individualism, albeit within a framework of non-aggressiveness. But even the prized and admired non-aggressiveness has a high price, and one that probably few people in the West would be prepared to pay: no deviation from the norm is tolerated. As Mead says, 'Those who suffer most among the Arapesh . . . are the violent, aggressive men, and the violent, aggressive woman', but *the man suffers a little less than the women*.

'By the insistence that all people are good and gentle, that men and women alike are neither strongly nor aggressively sexed [note this, those who plead for women's aggressive' sexuality], that no one has any other motive except to grow yams and children, the Arapesh have made it im-possible to formulate rules for properly controlling those whose temperaments do not conform to the accepted ideal.'

The price for Utopia, scarcely mentioned in the books, but

certainly very much in the awareness of Mead herself, who ends her study on the following note of sanity:

> 'It is hard to judge which seems to us the most Utopian and unrealistic behaviour, to say that there are no differences between men and women, or to say that both men and women are naturally maternal, gentle, responsive and unaggressive.'

If Mead's Arapesh are somewhat unrealistically viewed by feminists as an ideal model for our society, the salient features of their opposite number, the Gusii, who have a higher incidence of rape than even we do, also tend to be glossed over by these writers. The Gusii, for example, like us, have no strong taboos attached to sex before marriage. I have yet to see feminists suggest however that we start surrounding sex with taboos of the same order as the Arapesh, for their double-thinking demands freedom from taboos as well as freedom from rape. The ethnographies that are selected to back up their case should be looked at cautiously, and in greater depth, for in most cases (as in the case of the Arapesh) only those features that back up some ideological point are selected. It is interesting, however, that the very omission of this crucial fact of sexual taboo versus non-taboo has brought home an important point which I will return to later, and which seems to get overlooked in the heated arguments on rape.

Many writers on the subject are capable of deploying both of Storr's propositions simultaneously—i.e., 'All men are rapists' and 'Society creates rapists'. Susan Brownmiller, for example, in *Against Our Will* makes both claims: she supports Amir who placed rape in the 'well-documented subcultures in which violence and aggression prevail', and stated 'there is no getting around the fact that most of those who engage in anti-social, criminal violence (murder, assault, rape and robbery) come from the lower socioeconomic classes', but says firmly in her introduction: 'What it all boils down to is that the human male can rape' . . . and it is 'human anatomy', an 'accident of biology', 'an accommodation requiring the locking together of two separate parts, penis into vagina' which 'may have been sufficient to have caused the creation of a male ideology of rape'. Well, which one is it, 'anatomy' (which is as good as saying 'innate') or 'social class'? You can't have it both ways. Other writers, such as Barbara Toner, have obviously been embarrassed by the Amir findings and his uneasy conclusion that rape is a lower-class crime and that aggressive and exploitative behaviour towards women is a phenomenon of the subculture of violence: 'However positive such a finding may seem on paper,' she claims, 'it is clearly not the case. Aggressive and exploitative behaviour is not peculiar to any socioeconomic group. It is displayed by men of all classes. Women from all classes can bear witness to the fact that they have been subjected to it.' She then blames the sample: 'Men with criminal backgrounds and men from lower socioeconomic groups generally are more likely to be arrested for anything than middle-class men. It is not unreasonable to assume that in the vast reservoir of unreported rapes and complaints dismissed by the police are countless middle-class rapists, immune by virtue of their blemish-free status.' So how are we to know? How are we to unravel any of the 'facts' about rape, the arguments being so bedevilled with 'invisible' facts on all sides?

Rape, as I have said, resembles mental illness in its chimerical quality; its definition changes depending on the place and the time. Marriage by capture in one society would become rape in ours; there are those in our society who would stretch the concept to include 'symbolic' rape, just as there is 'emotional' battering; and others—like Margaret Drabble, writing in *The Observer* on December 10, 1978—who would see it as an act of violence in the same category as having a nose or a jaw broken: 'Nobody wants to be raped . . . but then nobody wants to have his nose or jaw broken or all his teeth knocked out either ... If rape is a traumatic experience, I imagine that having one's teeth knocked out can be equally traumatic.' She asks, too, if rape should be treated as a special case: 'Should we not, in the name of freedom, resist the notion that rape is a special case?'

The separation between mind and body continues to be-devil the argument; whether 'violence' or 'consent' is the crucial issue—one is in the head, and one is in or on the body. It becomes increasingly difficult in a society which treats sex mechanistically, which dwells on the glories of friction and the penis, on orgasm and vibrators, where Erica Jong's heroines voluntarily use bottle-necks. The most oft-quoted literary extract in all the 'rape' arguments is the description of Tralala's rape in Hubert Selby's *Last Exit to Brooklyn*.

Many women, however, might feel equally dismayed and offended by Erica Jong's descriptions of her mechanical failures in bringing a lesbian lover to orgasm in *How to Save Your Own Life*. Her fantasies of the so-called sexually emanci-pated woman seem dangerously close in feeling to the 'survival of cunt-hatred' Germaine Greer deplores in *Last Exit*. Which brings us back again to the separation of mind and body, and why the question of rape today is more confused than ever, and why the 'all women ask for it' myth refuses to die and why rape remains so hard to prove, and procedure in a prosecution still so unpleasant in spite of recent legislation.

Questions of 'consent' or 'belief of consent' are in the head: they are hidden (or can be)—they are highly dependent on non-verbal behaviour: violence is visible; an act of sexual penetration is visible. The pleasurable sex act visibly may be undistinguishable from rape; it is only 'what is in the head', the emotions, the heart (or wherever one may wish to locate it) that transforms it from mere Masters and Johnson mechanics to an act of sexual intercourse with the stress on *intercourse*. That is why rape is a 'special case' whether we do or do not wish to attach a 'sexual mystic' to it, because it is an imitation, a cruel parody, of something most people hold the most private and cherished notions about. It will never be 'mere violence' for no-one in his right mind would have his teeth knocked out for pleasure, as we have sex for pleasure.

Sex and the sexual organs carry a multitude of meanings, even if, as emancipated women, we have what journalist Mary Kenny calls 'more robust' attitudes, and another factor that further confuses all the rape issues is that we have yet to work out and define this multitude of meanings. 'Virginity' may not exist as a norm, but 'symbolic' virginity—the notion that there is a precious, private part of herself a woman retains, to 'surrender' at some point to whomever she may choose—may. Sex for women may have ceased to be a 'shaming and horrible experience', women's virginity the prize property and status symbol of men, but most people draw up lines of demarcation somewhere, and even the most sexually emancipated women do not let their bodies take over completely but still exercise some control somewhere with the 'mind'. We live in a plural society; this is equally reflected in our sexual mores; some people continue to cling to taboos which others find out-moded; when we lump a multitude of offences under the headings of 'rape' we are throwing together a host of conflicting beliefs and standards, expectations and norms.

Much is couched in bodily language in our society; when men say 'there is no such thing as rape', they are cutting off beliefs from body, saying you can't have your cake and eat it— expressing their own fears about the Masters and Johnson takeover: if orgasm through clitoral stimulation has become the ultimate sexual experience whether found in vibrators, bottle-necks or anything else—if body can indeed exist as just body (the Shere Hite ideal)—what then is rape? If all after all is 'mechanics', how do we draw a line? When women say' All men are rapists' they are cutting off body from beliefs, or rather becoming *all* belief. A 'just' approach to rape would take into account the subjective viewpoints of both sides, for it would seem, there are few 'facts' about rape, only 'experiences'. The ancients were on much safer ground when they related rape to the marriage system or the purity system. Brownmiller is correct when she writes 'Today's young rapist has no thought of capturing a wife or securing an inheritance or estate. His is an act of impermanent conquest, not a practical approach to ownership and control', but she ought to go on to ask why this 'basic male-female struggle' persists even in societies where 'de-sexist' attitudes and actions are relatively well advanced and models of 'machismo' fast fading. Would a moral or psychic division of labour on the lines of the Arapesh be the answer? Are we really willing to learn the lessons they teach us about true reciprocity?

CHAPTER 9

The Alternative Body

'Man is more than a "naked ape", more than a complex computer on legs, more than a behavioural organism of an elaborate type. These views of man are held by many people because they are thought to be scientific, but an adequate scientific theory of man must include his unique capacity for producing symbols, for making his life meaningful, and even dramatic ...'

Robert Bocock, *Ritual in Industrial Society*

'Our symbols are our dreams about ourselves and maybe the guardians of our collective image should be careful how they tread on our dreams.'

David Martin, *Tracts Against the Times*

Women in modern technological society suffer from lack of ritual; if any deprivation exists, it can be said to be that—'symbol starvation'. But in this anti-ritualistic age, because of the 'unique capacity' of the human animal to produce and use symbols, women are increasingly turning to the natural symbols of the body: the bodily metaphor reigns supreme; the whole human condition is being expressed in and through the body; just as previous ages have reduced all to 'humours', we reduce it to 'hormones'. 'Menstruation' and the 'menopause' are held to be the keys to life and gynaecology the key to fate. Just as a decade or so ago the 'pill' was hailed as a new saviour, hormone replacement therapy or, more drastically, hysterectomy and sterilization today are being used by an increasing number of women as an 'answer' to their lives in spite of the fact that adverse evidence exists to suggest that these procedures may in fact cause more problems than they cure (see 'Depression and Hysterectomy', *Lancet* 2, 430–433).

In her book *Natural Symbols*, in which she expanded her thesis that 'the organic system provides an analogy of the social system which, other things being equal, is used in the same way and understood in the same way all over the world', Mary Douglas warned that 'strongly subjective attitudes to society get coded through bodily symbols'. She came to the conclusion that it was 'the study of everyone to preserve their vision from the constraints of the natural symbols when judging any social situation'.

She urged people too to 'cherish categories', for categories help us to order our lives symbolically. Unfortunately it seems to be very difficult for women to do just this when assessing their social situation. The Women's Lib movement has been largely anti-ritualistic and, because of its Marxist bias, inimical, even disparaging, towards symbolism generally, underestimating man's and woman's unique need for symbolic consonance. In its efforts to de-mythologise, it has tended to create new mythologies which couch everything in the natural symbols of the body. Thus 'fat' becomes a 'feminist issue',[1] 'rape' becomes symbolic, and so on. It is apt here to refer to Basil Bernstein's distinction between elaborated and restricted codes. Elaborated speech is where the speaker selects from a wide range of syntactic alternatives, which are flexibly organized; this requires complex planning but is relatively free of the social structure. In restricted speech, the speaker draws from a much narrower range of syntactic alternatives but it is deeply enmeshed in the social structure, serving to reinforce it. Thus the command 'Do this, because I'm your mother,' uses the restricted code; whereas 'Be quiet because I have a headache and you ought to be more considerate,' uses the elaborated code. The relevant point here is that the restricted code makes use of condensed symbols and is closer to *ritualism*, serving similar psychological and metaphoric functions.

Using this distinction, one could say that feminism speaks in the elaborated code: it shows a distinct lack of sensitivity to condensed symbols.

In the words of R. Bocock, and as many other anthropologists have shown, 'Ritual can integrate bodily feelings and

---

[1] Susan Orbach, *Fat is a Feminist Issue*. The author presents a most illogical argument. If fat were really dependent on women's deprived position in society, and all women were deprived, all women would be fat.

emotions with rational social purposes, and can thus go some way to healing the splits between the body and the intellect.' Furthermore, we know that 'without rituals life becomes utilitarian, technocratic and cold, devoid of human emotions'. Ritual can counteract the fragmentation produced by technological society and consciousness, for not only does it relate us to our own bodies in sutble ways, but also to other people. When we look at women in 'alternative societies' such as religious sects or communes who have found new meaning, enrichment and expression in traditional or ethnic symbols, we find, too, that they usually have fewer 'body problems'. They no longer use the direct language of the body, except in a highly ritualized way. Amongst my Hassidic group, depression, premenstrual and the menopausal syndrome had no place or meaning; there were other channels for expression whether through dance, song, prayer or special tasks (*'mitzvot'*); women in this society suffer no 'problem of meaning'; their carefully controlled, explicitly delineated environment linked them not only to their community, to the world, but to the universe as a whole, providing 'cosmic' as well as communal connections.

The dismal inventory of some of the leading feminist's battles with their own bodies—the depressions, the abortions, the dysmenorrhea, the painful labours, the weight problems, menopausal horrors—provide a sad statement of cosmic *disconnection*; they have lost, abandoned, thrown away their symbols, and the price they pay is their own body. To use Shulamith Firestone's much quoted description of birth as 'shitting a pumpkin', illustrates very well the movement's tendency to reduce everything to its physical husk with no sensitivity to the symbol itself. Adrienne Rich describes herself in *Of Woman Born* as both literally and metaphorically 'allergic to pregnancy', and after her third child was born, decided to be sterilised. Germaine Greer has made her gynaeological problems common knowledge. She is no doubt describing her own early experiences of menstruation in *The Female Eunuch* when she writes:

> '. . . no little girl who finds herself bleeding from an organ which she didn't know she had until it began to incommode her, feels that nature is a triumph of design and that whatever is, is right. When she discovers that the pain attending this horror is in some way her *fault*, the result of improper adaptation to her female role, she really feels like the victim of a bad joke.'

The passage displays Puritanism most of all, and the fact that not all little girls experience menstruation this way is proved by the wealth of anthropological material which suggests that to many, on the contrary, it is a source of real pride. Many women from rigidly Puritanical backgrounds, however, do, and this remains unfortunate as it colours all their later experiences, and may prevent them ever coming to terms with their bodies or indeed translate into a rejection of female role.

To some extent the counter-culture of the 'Back to Nature' brigade, alternative medicine, 'nature-birth', encounter groups and yoga enthusiasts, has attempted to provide new rituals (or has tried to re-incorporate bits and pieces from traditional systems), has tried to salvage the wreckage; but the counter-culture is by its nature doomed to relative failure as the dominant culture, that of technology, is so all pervasive. The counter-culture tends to produce its own symbols which are largely unrelated to any wider social whole or historical context; thus we arrive at the 'surfeit of symbols' mostly of a 'private' nature which I described in the chapter on pollution; the heavy leaning on Jung or psycho-analytic theory which is relatively a-social and a-historical.

The counter-culture is hampered, too, except for the few who find total religious commitment in the traditional sense, by a lack of ideological framework in which to vi ew man's fate, life and death, which can mean again that people have to create their own rituals unrelated to a more meaningful whole. The 'nothingness' of death has affected our attitudes towards all the other major rites de passage, especially menstruation and birth: it provides a sombre background to all our thoughts. Each day I exercise to a taped song which proclaims over and over again, 'Take care of your Body. It's the only one, the only one you've got.' There is a desperation about that line which strikes me each time.

Left only with a mechanistic model of man, and a consciousness which is predominantly technological, it has become increasingly difficult to give meaning to other areas of life; the Women's Movement has, largely speaking, embraced technology and put paid to traditional symbols, but it has done little in the way of providing a new framework to 'connect' women to the world. By advocating the breakdown of the traditional division of labour between the sexes and the corresponding mutuality that traditionally produced, the Women's Movement has shown an immense insensitivity to condensed symbols generally. By putting, in the most mechanistic sense possible, only one chromosome between male and female, the essential brick at the base of an immensely complex symbolic system has been pulled out and toppled the whole pyramid. Women instead have switched to the more dangerous natural symbols of the body: the music gone, only a dull clatter and a few screams remain.

The only discourse, it seems, now open to women, is largely a gynaecological one. Deprived of a medium for expression, they are driven to the ultimate denial and nihilism of sterilization. It has been the symbolic act par excellence of our age. Professor Norman Morris of the Hammersmith Hospital, London, wrote the following in 1976. Since then sterilization has increased tremendously as a popular form of birth control.

'There is an unusual group of women who seek sterilization

as a rejection of their own femininity. They see their un-happiness and depression as entirely related to the problems that result from being a housewife and a mother. The privation, the boredom, the irritabilities, all stem from being a woman and they seek to renounce their role and thereby gain release from their misery. *Many fail to realize that sterilization cannot bring the immediate release they are seeking.* [my emphasis].

I hesitate to leave the argument on such a note of gloom, even though sociology has been described as deeply negative, and compared in *The Homeless Mind* (Peter L. Berger et al) to Goethe's Mephistopheles, a 'spirit that ever says no'.

Can an alternative body of belief be said to exist for women, free from the ever-lapping waves of technological consciousness, mechanisticity and the new myths that these have generated?

As we flick through the glossy magazines at the hairdresser, apply our make-up, heed our diets, do our exercises, make love, have our babies, mourn our loved ones, suffer our pains and joys, and just live out our day to day lives, what can we do to be more free, more at ease with those bodies, those outward shells of our existence? First, awareness: we can look around and see what life offers. Of course, in a plural society, there is not *one* alternative body of belief, but several; but out of the patchwork quilts of varying lifestyles, can we see some that work better than others? 'Work' in the sense of providing some degree of consonance on all levels for their practitioners, some degree of harmony between mind and body. What we learn about the 'ideal' alternative body is somewhat paradoxical and perhaps even unwelcome. There are no El Dorados, but women in well-defined communities, with well-defined roles and well-defined expressive outlets (i.e., ritual), with an organic as opposed to mechanistic view of the body, appear to suffer less fragmentation than women in poorly-defined communities, with poorly-defined roles and little expressive

outlet: women who dance, pray and work in whatever sense—
I do not distinguish voluntary from paid work—women in
fact who *participate*. What we are talking about to some extent
is the difference between 'Gemeinschaft'—those communal
relations based on deep levels of emotion and feeling, and
'Gesellschaft', relations such as those found in modern industrial societies and based on rational calculation. The
former exists in peasant societies, religious communities and a
few ethnic urban pockets, and the latter is a condition of urban
living. Sociologists and anthropologists have used many
different terms to describe the differences between the two
sets of organization and of life style. One side, however,
usually implies harmonious interrelatedness, the other fragmentation or anomie, as Durkheim termed it. Fritjof Capra
came to the conclusion that in the physical sciences the organic
view was the more fundamental—the one that regards all
phenomena in the universe as integral parts of an inseparable,
'harmonious whole', while not denying that the mechanistic
one was still useful for coping with the everyday environment
of technology. He concludes that

> 'The world view implied by modern physics is inconsistent
> with our present society, which does not reflect the har-
> monious interrelatedness we observe in nature. To achieve
> such a state of dynamic balance, a radically different
> social and economic structure will be needed: a cultural
> revolution in the true sense.'

The time has come to change our paradigm; but since it
would be unrealistic and retrograde to suppose that we could
do away with modern technology altogether as some counter-
modernists have advocated, we cannot envisage the emergence
of totally new social forms, as these are largely, and will continue to be, technologically determined. What we can do,
however, is recognize and hang on to whatever is valuable and

enriching in what we have: we should resist being seduced by arguments that encourage us to ditch all remnants of ritual; it is the most underestimated commodity we have, and one of the only safeguards of our humanity. The Women's Liberation movement, based as it is on Marxism, makes itself unnecessarily restrictive by leaving out man's symbolic life. Ritual can provide the sense of harmony, unity and wholeness like nothing else can; it does so by working with the whole of the person; it articulates ways of finding resolutions to the problem of meaning and evil. Human beings need to relate to one another in the heights and depths of experience and ritual can provide such a way. In Erich Fromm's definition it is 'shared action expressive of common strivings rooted in common values'. (emphasis mine).

The counter-culture has attempted to create new communities with their own rituals which largely have been short-lived. It must not be forgotten, however, that women as 'marginals' are, and always have been the supreme counter-culture; this has been their greatest strength. As Elise Boulding writes in *Women in the Twentieth-Century World*,

> 'The power of the marginals lies precisely in their lack of at-homeness in the world in which they live. Because they do not "belong" in the sense that they are never invited into society's back rooms where decisions that shape their lives are made, because they are usually treated as Objects, never subjects of the social process, they are driven to affirm belonging at another level.'

In that sense the Women's Movement was correct in placing them with Jews and Blacks.

The Women's Movement has tried to persuade women to abandon the counter-culture and come on over into the mainstream technological culture. The family, for example, traditionally always provided the greatest bulwark against an overly institutionalized, bureaucratized world, that existed—

women are now being persuaded that institutionalized 'day-care nurseries' must take over from the family, as must 'real' work of factory or office from 'unreal' work of the home. When women become technocrats then we are surely doomed!

When woman, in the old scheme of things, was put on the side of the 'Wild,' Art, mysticism, irrationality, gentleness, Beauty or whatever, it was a symbolic expression of her ability to 'resist' society, to stay a 'marginal'; the 'Eternal Feminine' was the eternal outsider, and I for one, would never wish to relinquish that position.

BIBLIOGRAPHY

Amir, Menachem. *Patterns in Forcible Rape*. University of Chicago Press, 1971

Ardener, Shirley, ed. *Perceiving Women: Essays in Anthropology*. Routledge & Kegan Paul, 1975

Ballinger, S. 'The Role of Psychosocial Stress in Menopausal Symptoms', the Fifth International Congress of Psychosomatic Obstetrics and Gynaecology, Nov. 1977

Barthes, Roland. *Mythologies*. Paladin, 1973

Beels, Christine. *The Childbirth Book*. Turnstone Books, 1978

Berger, John. *Ways of Seeing*. Penguin, 1972

Berger, Peter L., Berger, Brigitte, and Kellner, Hansfried. *The Homeless Mind*. Penguin, 1977

Bernstein, Basil. *A Socio-Linguistic Approach to Social Learning*: Penguin Survey of the Social Sciences, ed. J. Gould. Penguin, 1965

Bocock, R. *Ritual in Industrial Society: A sociological analysis of ritual in modern England*. Allen & Unwin, 1974

Boulding, Elise. *Women in the Twentieth Century World*. Sage Publications, 1974.

Bowskill, Derek, and Linacre, Anthea. *The Male Menopause*. Frederick Muller, 1976

Breen, Dana. *The Birth of a First Child*. Tavistock, 1975

Brook, Danaë. *Naturebirth: Preparing for natural birth in an age of technology*. Heinemann, 1976

Brown, G. V., and Harris, T. *Social Origins of Depression: A study of psychiatric disorder in women*. Tavistock, 1978

Brownmiller, Susan. *Against Our Will*. Penguin, 1976

Capra, Fritjof. *The Tao of Physics*. Fontana, 1976

Cohen, Mabel Blake. 'Personal Identity and Sexual Identity', in Miller, Jean Baker, ed., *Psychoanalysis and Women*

Comfort, Alex. *A Good Age*. Mitchell Beazley, 1977

De Beauvoir, Simone. *The Second Sex*. Penguin, 1972

——,——. *Old Age*. Penguin, 1977

Douglas, Mary. *Purity and Danger*. Penguin, 1970

——,——. *Natural Symbols*. Penguin, 1973

——,——. *Implicit Meanings: Essays in Anthropology*. Routledge & Kegan Paul, 1975

Eliade, Mircea. *Myths, Dreams and Mysteries*. Fontana, 1972

Friedman, R. J., and Katz, M. M., eds. *The Psychology of Depression*. John Wiley, 1974

German, G. A. *Aspects of Clinical Psychiatry in Sub-Saharan Africa*. 1972

Gilder, George. *Sexual Suicide*. Millington, London, 1973

Gorer, Geoffrey. *Death, Grief and Mourning in Contemporary Britain*. Cresset Press, 1965

Greer, Germaine. *The Female Eunuch*. Paladin, 1971

Hite, Shere. *Sexual Honesty*. Warner Books, 1974

——,——. *The Hite Report: A nationwide study on female sexuality*. Wildwood House, 1977

Holbrook, David. *Sex and Dehumanisation*. Pitman, 1972

Hoover, Robert, Gray, Laman A., Cole, Philip, and Mac-Mahon, Brian. 'Menopausal Estrogen and Breast Cancer', *New England Journal of Medicine*, August 1976
Howell, Georgina. *In Vogue*. Penguin, 1975
Hudson, Liam. *The Cult of the Fact*. Jonathan Cape, 1972

Illich, Ivan. *Limits to Medicine*. Penguin, 1977

Jong, Erica. *How to Save Your Own Life*. Panther, 1978

Kempe, Ruth S., and Kempe, Henry C. *Child Abuse*. Fontana, 1978
Kitzinger, Sheila. *The Experience of Childbirth*. Penguin, 1978
——,——. *Women as Mothers*. Fontana, 1978

Lévi-Strauss, Claude. *Man, Culture and Society*. Oxford University Press, 1956
——,——. *The Savage Mind*. Weidenfeld, 1966
Levine, Robert A. 'Gusi Sex Offences: A Study in social control', *Amer. Anthrop.*, Vol. 6, 1959
Lewis, Ioan. *Social Anthropology in Perspective*. Penguin, 1976
Liedloff, Jean. *The Continuum Concept*. Futura, 1975

Martin, David. *Tracts against the Times*. Lutterworth Press, 1973
Masters, W. H., and Johnson, V. E. *Human Sexual Response*. Little, Brown, 1966
Mead, Margaret. *Male and Female*. Pelican, 1962
——,——. *Sex and Temperament in Three Primitive Societies*. Routledge & Kegan Paul, 1977
Miller, Jean Baker. *Psychoanalysis and Women*. Penguin, 1973
Morley, Sheridan. *Marlene Dietrich*. Elm Tree Books, 1976
Morris, N., and Arthure, H. *Sterilization*. Peter Owen, 1976

Nilson, A. 'Paranatal Emotional Adjustment: A prospective investigation of 165 women', *Acta Psychiat. Scand.*, Suppl. 220, 1970

Orbach, Susan. *Fat is a Feminist Issue*. Paddington Press, 1978

Perutz, Kathryn. *Beyond the Looking Glass: Life in the beauty culture*. Hodder & Stoughton, 1970

Prince, B. *The Changing Picture of Depressive Syndromes in Africa*, 1968

Rapoport, Rhona and Robert. *Dual Career Families*. Penguin, 1971

Renvoize, Jean. *Children in Danger: The causes and prevention of baby battering*. Routledge & Kegan Paul, 1974

Rich, Adrienne. *Of Woman Born*. Virago, 1977

Seligman, Martin P. *See* Friedman, R. J. and Katz, M. M., *The Psychology of Depression*.

Shuttle, Penelope, and Redgrove, Peter. *The Wise Wound*. Gollancz, 1978

Slater, E. and Cowrie, V. *The Genetics of Mental Disorders*. London University Press, 1971

Sommer, Robert. *Personal Space: The behavioural basis of design*. Prentice-Hall, 1969

Sontag, Susan. *Against Interpretation and other essays*. Eyre & Spottiswoode, 1967

Sperber, Dan. *Re-thinking Symbolism*. Cambridge University Press, 1975

Stassinopoulos, Arianna. *The Female Woman*. Fontana, 1974

Storr, Anthony. *Human Aggression*. Penguin, 1971

Sutherland, Stuart. *Breakdown: A personal crisis and medical dilemma*. Weidenfeld, 1976

Toner, Barbara. *The Facts of Rape*. Arrow, 1977

Turner, Victor. *The Forest of Symbols*. Cornell University Press, 1967

Walker, Alexander. *The Celluloid Sacrifice: Aspects of sex in the movies*. Michael Joseph, 1966

Weideger, Paula. *Female Cycles*. The Women's Press, 1978

Wilson, Robert A. *Feminine Forever*. M. Evans, 1966

Wing, J. K. *Reasoning about Madness*. Oxford University Press, 1978

Wolff, Charlotte. *Bisexuality*. Quartet, 1978

Index

Abuse, Abused Body,
  and aggression, 123–4, 127, 130;
  and deprivation, 124, 127–8; and
  social class, 125–6, 133–4; as non-
  verbal communication, 128–30; and
  the Arapesh, 130–3; and 'consent'
  to rape, 135–7
Against Our Will, 122, 124, 133
Ageing, Ageing Body, 14, 47, 85;
  and our attitude towards, 86, 88;
  and the menopause, 86–93, 100;
  and the 'sexual forever' woman,
  94–7; and death, 97–8; and
  uselessness, 98–101
Aggression, 29, 123–4, 127, 132–3, 134
Aggressive response, 127
Agoraphobia, 109
Albany Trust, 34–5
Alcoholism, 8
Alternative Body, The, 138–47
Alternative societies, 141, 142
Amir, Menachem, 124, 133, 134
Androcentrism, 16–17
Androgyny, 36, 59
Anger, 119
Angst, 12, 65
Anima, animus, 36
Ante-natal classes, 68, 74–5, 77, 82,
  116–17; author's teaching in, 23, 69,
  74, 115, 119
Anti-depressants, 105
Anti-ponography, 17
Arapesh, the, 62, 130–3, 137

*Aspects of Clinical Psychiatry in Sub-
  Saharan Africa*, 107n

Ballinger, S., 92
Bardot, Brigitte, 44
Bar-mitzvah, 65
Barthes, Roland, 45
Battering, 8, 56, 123, 124–30;
  battered child syndrome, 124; as
  non-verbal communication, 129–20
Beauty culture, 8, 9, 10, 14, 41, 48
Beels, Christine, 66
Behaviourist school, 119
Bereshit Rabba, 36
Berger, John, 39, 40, 41
Berger, Peter, 14–15, 19, 72, 78–80, 144
Berlei, 23
Bernstein, Basil, 140
Beyond the Looking Glass, 39, 41
Biofeedback, 119
Biological determinism, 29
Biological rhythms, 9
Birth, Birthing Body, 14, 24, 30–1, 51,
  59, 66, and psychoprophylaxis, 9,
  65; and rituals, 20, 143; and
  modernization, 67–9; naturebirth,
  65, 67, 69, 71, 84, 142; and
  Caesarian section, 68, 69; and
  Leboyer, 69–73; and fathers, 73–6;
  and bonding, 76–7, and cults, 77;
  and expectations of mother, 78–82;
  and mortality rates, 82; and rites
  de passage, 83–4

Birth of a First Child, The, 30–2
Birth-control, *see* Contraception
Birth-trauma, 61
Bisexuality, 17, 29, 33–8
Blodeuwedd, 43
Blurred Body, The, 22;
    and changing shape, 23–4; and
    sexism, 24–5; and exchange, 25–8;
    and feminisation of males, 28–9;
    and masculinity/feminity, 29–31;
    and woman's space, 32–3; and
    bisexuality, 33–8
Bocock, Robert, 138, 140–1
Body awareness, 9–12, 65, 73, 117
Bonding, 76–7
Bott, Dr Michael, 87–8
Boulding, Elise, 146
Bowie, David, 37
Bowskill, Derek, 87
Brave New Baby, 22
Breakdown, 21
Breakdown, 104–5
Breakdown in society, 8
Breasts, 15, 17, 40, 43; breast feeding,
    30, 31, 76; cancer of the, 91–2
Breen, Dana, 30–2, 37
Briccolage, 73, 73n
Brook, Danae, 66
Brown, G. W., 113
Brownmiller, Susan, 122, 124, 133, 137
Bruch, J. C., 91
Byrd, B. F. Jr., 91

Caesarian section, 68, 69
Cancer, 91–2
Cant, Joan, 127
Capra, Fritjof, 26–7, 145
Cartesian thought, 37
Categories, 140, 140n
Cell 'sauvage', 72
*Changing Picture of Depressive Syndromes
    in Africa*, 107n
Charcot, 104
Chat-shows, 19
Child abuse, 123, 124–30
Child Abuse, 122, 123, 126
Childbirth, *see* Birth
Childbirth Book, The 66
Children in Danger, 124–5, 129
China, 93

Cognitive systems, 72
Cohen, Mabel Blake, 25–6
Cole, Philip, 91
Comfort, Alex, 86, 99
Componentiality, 15
Confinement, home, 67, 68, 68n, 72,
    81; hospital, 68, 68n, 72
Contamination, 108
Continuum Concept, The, 128, 128n
Contraception. 14, 24, 59, 62, 80
Cosmetic surgery, 14
Cosmology, 14
Counter-culture, 11
Counter-modernization, 67
Couples, 74–5, 76, 77
Couvade, 74, 74n
Cowrie, V., 103n
Crawford, Betty, 42
Cults, 77

Dance, 120
Davis, Adele, 84
Day care nurseries, 24, 146–7
De Beauvoir, Simone, 17, 88, 94, 95,
    96, 98–9
De Chardin, Teilhard, 31
Deacon, Anthony, 37n
Death, 11, 19, 47, 60, 61, 62, 65, 73,
    82–3, 86, 88–9, 97–9, 143
*Death, Grief and Mourning in Contemporary
    Britain*, 85, 97–8
Dependency, 25–6, 31
Dependent needs, 26
Depression, Depressed Body, 141;
    as substitute for hysteria, 104–5,
    109–10; reasons for, 105–7; link
    with emancipation, 107; and
    personal space, 107–9, 110–13, 115,
    116, 119, 120–1; and spirit
    possession, 109–10; and
    environment, 113–15; and social
    structure, 115–16; and diet, 117;
    and social iatrogenesis, 118; and
    emotional outlets, 119; and psycho-
    therapy, 119–20; and dancing, 120
    see also Post-natal depression;
    Menopausal depression; Psychotic
    depression, Pathological depression
'Depression and Hysterectomy', 139
Deprivation, 107, 124, 127–8, 139

Dick-Read, Grantley, 68, 69
Diet; fads, 10; supplements, 89;
  wholefood, 117
Dietrich, Marlene, 41, 42, 43, 47, 95
Division of labour, 143
Double consciousness, 78–80
Douglas, Professor Mary, 10, 45, 54–6,
  57, 74, 96, 108, 127–8, 139–40
Drabble, Margaret, 134–5
Drugs, 8, 86, 87, 89–91, 92–3, 105, 112
Dual Career Families, 32
Durkheim, Emile, 8, 145
Dysmenorrhea, 30, 141

Elaborated code, 140
Eliade, Mircea, 36, 51, 61, 63
Emotional outlets, 119
Employment, 8, 24
Encounter groups, 83, 142
Epidural, 69
Equal opportunities, 8, 24
'Eternal Feminine, The', 47, 147
Exchange, 24–5, 26–7, 33, 34, 35, 38,
  95
Exorcist, The, 52

Facts of Rape, The, 124
Family, 24, 106, 146–7
Family breakdown, 100
Fashion, 23
Fat is a Feminist Issue, 140, 140n
Fathers, 23, 73–6
Female Cycles, 50, 58, 60, 61, 69–70,
  91–2, 93
Female Eunuch, The, 46–7, 95–6, 141–2
Female Woman, The, 97
'Feminine Forever', 86, 94–7
Feminine Forever, 89–90
Feminine role, 26
Femininity, 30–1, 36, 37, 38
Feminisation of male role, 28–9
Feminism, 12, 24, 30, 33, 46, 51, 55,
  56, 126, 140, 141
Film stars, 41, 42–4
Firestone, Shulamith, 141
Fostering, 100
Fragmentation, 13–14, 81, 84, 100,
  141, 144, 145
Freud, Sigmund, 103, 123, 129
Friction, 15, 135

Fromm, Eric, 146
Fuller, Nancy, 78

Garbo, 40, 42, 43, 45, 47
Geertz, Hildred, 58
Gematria, 53, 53n
Gemeinschaft, 115, 145
Gender identity, 29, 37
Genetics of Mental Disorders, 103n
German, G. A., 107n
Gerocomy, 95
Gesellschaft, 145
Gestalt therapy, 9
Gilder, George, 28–9
Glamour, Glamorous Body, 39;
  the glamour myth, 40–2, 47–8;
  glamour girls, 43–5; and health
  cults, 46; and feminism, 46, 48; and
  symbols, 48; and morality, 48–9
Glynn, Prudence, 23
God, 36
Gorer, Geoffrey, 85, 97–8
Gray, Laman A., 91
Greer, Germaine, 27, 40, 46–7, 48, 51,
  58, 95–6, 135, 141–2
Grodder, George, 61
Gusii, 133
Gynaecologist, 69–71
Gynaecology, 8, 21, 139

Halsell, Grace, 93
Harlow, Jean, 42
Harris, T., 113
Hassidim, 10, 27, 48, 58–9, 60–1,
  64–5, 120, 141
Hayworth, Rita, 44
Health cults, 45–6
Hepburn, Katharine, 42
Hinduism, 35–6
Hite, Shere, 15, 34, 38
Hite Report, 15–17, 136
Holbrook, David, 17
Holland, studies in, 81, 82
Hollywood, 42–3
Holy Grail, the, 52–3
Holzer, Baby Jane, 44
Homeless Mind, The, 14–15, 144
Homosexuality, 37, 38
Hoover, Robert, 91–2

Hormones, 87, 88, 89, 90–1, 93, 97, 139; replacement therapy, 86, 89, 90–1, 139; reductionism, 87; deprivation theory, 92
Housework, 33
How to Save Your Own Life, 135
Hudson, Liam, 18
Hughes, Howard, 43
Human Aggression, 127
Hung, Dr Wellington, 109
Hysterectomy, 139
Hysteria, 103–5, 109–10, 116

Identity: conflict, 26; problems, 34, 35, 37, 47; crisis, 38, 76
Illich, Ivan, 11, 12n, 20, 88–9, 118
Implicit Meanings, 74
Impotence, 88
Incest, 123
Infant mortality, 78, 82
Interchange, 27
Intercourse, 16, 17–18
Interdependency, 25, 26

Johnson, Masters and, 17–19, 135, 136
Jong, Erica, 17, 135
Jordan, Brigitte, 78
Judaism, 36
Jung, C., 27, 36, 48, 51, 65, 142
Jung, Emma, 53

Kabbalism, 27, 35–6, 53, 59
Kempe, R. S. and C. H., 122, 123, 124, 126
Kenny, Mary, 13, 136
Kitzinger, Sheila, 68, 70, 71, 73, 78, 81–2
Kroll, Una, 35, 36, 37

La Fontaine, Jean, 60
Labour, 68, 72, 74–5; active management of, 67–9
Laing, R. D., 77, 106
Language, 11–12, 20, 21, 141
Language and Silence, 102
Last Exit to Brooklyn, 135
Laver, James, 42
Layard, John, 102
Leach, Edmund, 85
Leboyer, Frederick, 69, 70–3, 77, 84

Lesbians, 17, 61–2
Lévi-Strauss, Claude, 25, 51–2, 66
Lewis, I. M., 98, 109–10
Liedloff, Jean, 128
Life-cycle, 11, 31, 34
Limits to Medicine, 20, 118
Linacre, Anthea, 87
Liqqutei Amarim, 113n
Love, 16, 17, 37, 92–3
Lubavitch Hassidim, 113–14, 115
Lyman, 108

Mackenzie, Midge, 48
MacMahon, Brian, 91
Make-overs, 43–4
Make-up, 43, 44, 45, 46
Male and Female, 27–8
Male dominance, 56
Male menopause, 87–8, 100
Male Menopause, The, 87
Male space, 49, 112
Man, Culture and Society, 25
Maoris, 55
Marriage, 24, 33, 59, 76, 124
Marriage guidance, 19
Martin, David, 138
Masculinity, 28–9, 30–1, 36, 37, 38
Masters and Johnson, 17–19, 135, 136
Maternal mortality, 82
Maximilization, 15
Mead, Margaret, 27–8, 29, 62, 130–3
Measurability, 15
Mechanical Body, The, 13, 38, 86; and fragmentation, 14–15; and the Hite Report, 15–17; the ultimate mechanical body, 17–18; and problem solving, 19; and ritual, 20; and lack of language, 21
Mechanistic models, 11
Mechanisticity, 15, 16, 17, 37
Medicine, 14
Mediterranean societies, 49
Meir, Golda, 95
Menopause, 61, 62, 70, 87–8, 100, 139; and depression, 88, 92, 110, 141; mythology of, 89–90; and oestrogen therapy, 91–2; symptoms of, 92–3, 99
'Menopausal Estrogen and Breast Cancer', 91–2

Menstruation, 20, 51–65, 70, 72, 93, 139, 142, 143; menstrual blood, 51, 55, 60–1, 62; menstrual huts, 56, 130; menstrual taboos, 51, 54–8, 60–1, 62–3, 65, 70, 97, 130
Mental health, 14, 32, 35, 116
Mental illness, 8, 48, 77
  see also Depression
Middle age, 34
Midwife, 70, 78
'Mikvah', 57, 58–9, 61, 63–4, 112
Ministry of Marriage, 19
Models, 41, 44–5
Modernization, 67, 71, 81
Monroe, Marilyn, 41, 42
Morris, Desmond, 23–4
Morris, Professor Norman, 143–4
Mother-in-law, 77, 96
Mourning, 20
Muslim, women, 48, 49; society, 49
Mutuality, 11, 26, 31, 34, 123, 143
Myth, 21, 97; of glamour, 40–2, 45, 46–9; of menstruation, 53; of the menopausal woman, 86, 89–90; of the 'sexual forever' woman, 86, 93–6; of the male menopause, 87
Mythologies, 45
Mythology, 11–12, 65, 140

Naked Ape, The, 24
Natural Symbols, 127–8, 139–40
Nature, 12, 14, 67, 71, 72
Naturebirth, 66
Naturopaths, 81
Neophytes, 83
Neurasthenia, 110
Nilson, A., 30

Oestrogen, 89, 91, 92–3; replacement therapy, 89, 91–2
Of Woman Born, 7, 141
Old Age, 88
Open-plan design, 111
Oppression, 107
Orbach, Susan, 140n
Organic models, 11
Orgasm, 15–16, 17–18, 135, 136
Orwell, George, 13

Particle physics, 11

Pathological depression, 105
Patterns in Forcible Rape, 124
Penis, 15–16, 17, 29, 135
Perceiving Woman, 60
Periodicity, 52
Perls, Fritz, 106
'Personal Identity and Sexual Identity', 25n
Personal space, 107–9, 110–13, 116, 119, 120–1; see also Woman's space; Male space
Perutz, Kathryn, 39, 41, 42, 44
Photographs, 44–5
Physical fitness, 46
Pollution, Polluting Body, 50–2; and The Wise Wound, 52–3; and symbolism, 53–4, 60–5; and the Walbiri, 55; and menstrual taboos, 55, 56, 57–8, 62–4; and ritual baths, 57, 58–9, 63; and the lesbian commune, 61–2
Post-natal depression, 31, 105, 110, 113, 116–17
Pre-menstrual tension, 19, 58, 61, 105, 110, 118, 141
Pregnancy, 9, 25–6, 30, 32; pre-pregnancy, 25; post-partum, 25, 30, 32
Primitive societies, 14, 21, 29, 60, 74, 98, 106–7, 109–10
Primordial state, 36–7
Prince, B., 107n
Problem pages, 19
Problem phone-ins, 19
Problem solving inventiveness, 15, 16, 19
Psychiatric symptoms, 30
Psychiatry, 19
Psychoprophylaxis, 9, 65, 68, 73
Psychotic depression, 105
Puberty rites, 62–3
Punk, 40, 45, 46
Purity and Danger, 54, 108
Purity laws, 51, 57, 58–9

Quant, Mary, 45

Radical psychiatry, 106
Rambert, Marie, 95

Rape, 8, 29, 56, 123–7, 130, 133–7; date rape, 126; gang rape, 126; symbolic rape, 134, 140; consent to rape, 135–6
Rapoport, Rhona and Robert, 32
Reciprocity, 25
Redgrove, Peter, 52–3, 63–4
Religion, 19, 35–6, 86, 97–8, 104, 115–16, 120–1, 142
Renvoize, Jean, 124–5, 128, 129
Reproducibility, 15
Restricted code, 140
Rethinking Symbolism, 54
Retreats, 112–13, 120–1
Rich, Adrienne, 7, 51, 141
Rites de passage, 83, 143
Ritual, 14, 20–1, 36, 64–5, 83, 139, 140–1, 142, 144, 145–6
Ritual bath, see 'Mikvah'
Ritual in Industrial Society, 138
Road to Wigan Pier, The, 13
Rorvik, David, 22
Russell, Jane, 43

Savage Mind, The, 66
Scapegoat theory, 105–6
Schneur Zalman, Rabbi, 102, 113n
Schumacher, E. F., 11, 12n
Second-hand speech, 45
Selby, Hubert, 135
Selighan, Martin P., 120, 120n
Semen, 60
'Seven Steps to Stardom', 43
Sex, 34–5, 135–6
Sex and Dehumanisation, 17
Sex therapists, 35, 94
Sexism, 24
Sexocrats, 15
Sexologists, 17
Sexual division of labour, 24–5, 33
Sexual Honesty, 16–17
Sexual mores, 10
Sexual problems, 34
Sexual role, 24, 26, 27–9, 31, 32, 37, 55
Sexual spheres, 11
Sexual Suicide, 28–9
Sexual violation, 123
Sexuality, 15, 29, 35, 37, 61, 65, 94–5
Shaman, 19, 69–70, 71
'Shiva', 20

Shuttle, Penelope, 52–3, 63–4
Slater, E., 103n
Social anthropology, 9–10
Social Anthropology in Perspective, 98
Social class, 126, 133–4
Social iatrogenesis, 118, 128
Social Origins of Depression, 113
Social structure, 115–16
Socialist societies, 106
Somali Muslims, 109–10
Sommer, Robert, 108
Sontag, Susan, 40
Spare parts surgery, 89
Spare Rib, 24
Speech codes, 140
Sperber, Dan, 54
Spirit possession, 104, 109–10, 116
Stassinopoulos, Arianna, 97
Status, 49
Steinem, Gloria, 48
Steiner, George, 102
Sterilization, 139, 141, 143–4
Stiller, Mauritz, 43
Storr, Anthony, 127, 130, 133
Stress, 105, 107
Subculture of violence, 124, 126, 134
Superwoman, 49
Sutherland, Stuart, 104–5, 106
Swanson, Gloria, 95
Symbols, 10–11, 20, 21, 48, 83, 84; symbol starvation, 8, 139; menstrual symbolism, 51–4, 56, 60–1, 62, 65; symbols of the body, 139; condensed symbols, 140, 143; natural symbols, 140, 141, 143

Taboos, 19, 20; touching, 37; menstrual, 51, 54–8, 60–3, 65, 97, 130; death, 97; sexual, 97, 133, 136
Tanya, The, 102, 113, 113n
Tao of Physics, The, 26–7
Taoism, 35–6
Technological consciousness, 11
Tension line, 32
Therapies, 8; see also Gestalt therapy
Times, The, 23, 71
Tinkering attitude, 14–15, 89
Toner, Barbara, 124, 125, 134
Tracts Against the Times, 138

Traditional societies, 80, 86;
  see also Primitive societies
Tranquillizers, 105
Transcendental meditation, 109, 119
Transvestism, 36
Turner, Victor, 83
Tylor, Edward, 26

Unification of opposites, 27

Vadim, Roger, 44
Vagina, 15, 16
Van Gennep, 83
Vaugh, W. K., 91
Vibrators, 17, 94, 135, 136
Victorian women, 109, 110
Vilcabamba, 93
Violence, 29, 56
Virginity, 136
Vitamin E, 65, 117
Vogue, 39, 43, 44–5, 46
Von Daniken, 53
Von Sternberg, Josef, 43

Walbiri, The, 55
Warhol, Andy, 41
Ways of Seeing, 39, 41

Weideger, Paula, 50, 58, 60, 61, 62–3,
  69–70, 91–2, 93, 94
West, Mae, 95
Wilson, Robert A., 89–90
Wing, J. K., 104
Wise Wound, The, 52–3, 55
Witches, 86, 89–90, 93, 95, 96–7
Wittgenstein, 21
Wolff, Charlotte, 33
Wolfgang, Marvin, 126
Woman's Journal, 35, 37n
Woman's Own, 105
Woman's shape, 23–4
Woman's space, 31–2, 110–12, 114,
  115; *see also* Personal space
Women as marginals, 146–7
Women as Mothers, 78, 81–2
Women in the Twentieth Century World,
  146
Women's groups, 112
Women's Lib movement, 10–11, 48,
  90, 140, 143, 146–7
Woolf, Virginia, 70
Workshops, 17
Wright, Erna, 68

Yoga, 109, 119, 142

Zoroastrians, 57n